Student Freelancing 101

A Start-to-Finish Course to Becoming a Student Freelancer

STF

Student Freelancing 101

A Start-to-Finish Course to Becoming a Student Freelancer

by Amber Leigh Turner

ISBN: 978-1481116534

Presented by Students That Freelance.
http://www.studentsthatfreelance.com

Designed by Amber Leigh Turner.
http://www.januarycreative.com
http://www.amberturner.com

Dedication

To Steven, my amazing boyfriend:

For being there when freelancing times were tough, telling me things will get better.
For being there when freelancing times are good, telling me "I told you so."

Thank you for supporting me through all of my crazy ideas, including writing a book during my last semester of college. Seriously, what was I thinking?

Most importantly, thank you for being my biggest fan throughout the past eight-plus years. I'm lucky and blessed to call you my teammate.

To my loving parents:

Thank you for raising me to be a strong, independent, and motivated woman. I hope that I have made you proud with all of my crazy ideas, like starting a business in college.

Syllabus

So you want to become a freelancer while you are in school? Below is the outline to help get you there!

Dedication	5
Introduction	9

Lesson 1: Is Student Freelancing For You?   12
1.1 Lecture: What Is Student Freelancing?	14
1.2 Quiz: Are You Prepared to Be a Student Freelancer?	15
1.3 Exercise: Why Do You Want to Freelance as a Student?	17
1.4 Lecture: Benefits and Drawbacks as a Student Freelancer	19
1.5 Exercise: Exploring Fields of Freelancing	21
1.6 Exercise: Everyone's Situation is Different	23
1.7 Exercise: Priorities - Time and School Impact	24
1.8 Lecture: Not Quite Ready to Start Freelancing as a Student?	27
1.9 Exam! Are you ready to start your freelancing career as a student?	28

Lesson 2: Creating the Blueprint   32
2.1 Lecture: Looking at the Big Picture	34
2.2 Quiz: Have You Thought About These Things Yet?	35
2.3 Exercise: Getting Your Ideas on Paper	37
2.4 Exercise: Researching The Industry	39
2.5 Exercise: Finding a Mentor	42
2.6 Lecture: Financial Safety Net	44
2.7 Exercise: Developing the Business Plan	45
2.8 Exercise: Setting Up a Time Line	49
2.9 Exam! How well does your plan hold up?	52

Lesson 3: Legal Matters   56
3.1 Lecture: Staying on the Straight and Narrow	58
3.2 Lecture: Personal Name or Business Name?	59
3.3 Exercise: Brainstorming Business Names	61
3.4 Lecture: The Dreaded 'T' Word	63
3.5 Lecture: How and Why to Use Contracts	65
3.6 Exercise: Developing a Working Contract	66
3.7 Exam! Do you have all of your legal ducks in a row?	68

Lesson 4: Setting Up Shop   72
4.1 Exercise: Determining Your Services	74
4.2 Exercise: Discovering and Creating Your Ideal Client Profile and Target Market	75
4.3 Quiz: How Well Do You Really Know Your Potential Clients?	77
4.4 Lecture: The All-Important Portfolio	80
4.5 Exercise: Getting Your Portfolio in Order	82
4.6 Exercise: Creating Your Work (and Life) Schedule	84
4.7 Exercise: Getting Your Office Organized	85

4.8 Lecture: Creating and Keeping Good Records   87

4.9 Exam! Is your office all in order?   89

Lesson 5: Show Me The Money!   92

5.1 Exercise: How Much Should You Charge?   94

5.2 Lecture: How To Properly Estimate Pricing for Projects   98

5.3 Exercise: Creating Proposals and Estimates for Clients   100

5.4 Quiz: How Good Are You At Creating Budgets (and Sticking To Them)?   102

5.5 Exercise: Giving Your Freelancing (and You) A Budget   103

5.6 Exercise: Setting Up Your Money Management System   105

5.7 Lecture: Invoicing Clients   107

5.8 Lecture: Accounting Practices for Freelancers   108

5.9 Exam! Are you ready to make some serious moolah?   109

Lesson 6: Getting Ready to Launch   112

6.1 Exercise: Developing Your Identity   114

6.2 Lecture: Your Website   115

6.3 Exercise: Getting Your Website Ready for Prime Time   117

6.4 Quiz: Double Check Everything   119

6.5 Exercise: Promoting Your Freelancing Before the Big Launch   123

6.6 Exercise: Launching Your Freelance Business   124

Lesson 7: Scream From The Rooftops (Marketing)   128

7.1 Lecture: An Overview of Marketing for Freelancers   130

7.2 Exercise: Developing a Marketing Plan   132

7.3 Exercise: Fine-Tuning and Updating Your Website   134

7.4 Lecture: Social Media, Advertising, Networking and Word-of-Mouth   135

7.5 Exercise: Developing Your Network   138

7.6 Exercise: Finding and Getting Your First Client   139

7.7 Exam! What all have you learned about marketing as a student freelancer?   141

Lesson 8: Working With Clients   144

8.1 Lecture: Communication Skills   146

8.2 Lecture: Professionalism   147

8.3 Lecture: Meeting Your First Client   148

8.4 Exercise: Creating Your Client Tracking System   149

8.5 Lecture: Spotting the Good, the Bad, and the Ugly Clients   152

8.6 Quiz: Client Do's and Don'ts   154

8.7 Lecture: Dealing with the Student Factor with Clients   157

8.8 Exercise: Oh no! Dealing With Unhappy Clients   159

8.9 Lecture: Getting Client Testimonials   160

8.10 Exam! Are you a whiz at dealing with your freelance clients?   162

Lesson 9: The Best of Both Worlds: Student and Freelancer   166

9.1 Lecture: Working During the Semester vs. During the Summer   168

9.2 Lecture: Keeping the School/Freelance/Life Balance 170

9.3 Lecture: Benefits of the "Student" Status 171

9.4 Lecture: Finding Ways to Intermingle School and Freelance 172

9.5 Exam! Know all the ins and outs of freelancing as a student? 173

Acknowledgements 206

About the Author: Amber Leigh Turner 207

Personal Notes 208

Lesson 10: The Next Steps In Your Freelancing Career **178**

10.1 Exercise: Evaluating Your Success 180

10.2 Lecture: Staying Organized Through the Fast & Slow Times 183

10.3 Lecture: Specializing and Finding a Niche 184

10.4 Lecture: When Should You Start Increasing Your Fees? 185

10.5 Exercise: Setting Goals for the Future 186

10.6 Lecture: Can't Handle the Load? When to Start Collaborating 189

10.7 Quiz: 10 Successful Habits of Student Freelancers 191

10.8 Lecture: Should You Continue Freelancing or Find A Full-Time Job? 192

10.9 Lecture: Starting and Working on Personal Side Projects 194

10.10 Exam! Ready to take your freelancing up a notch? 195

Special Goodies **200**

Conclusion: Wishing You Well Wishes! 202

Resources 203

Introduction

Over five years ago, I was like you, pondering the idea of freelancing. I surfed the Internet for hours, learning all I could. I talked to friends and family about what they thought about me freelancing while I was in school. I wanted to explore this fascinating new form of employment, but was unsure.

Like most freelancers, I fell into freelancing. I was presented with a couple of design opportunities from my (then) current employer and my (then) future employer, at the same time. Hunting around on the Internet, I was trying to find out how to handle these opportunities and how much to charge, all of which led me to one conclusion: people do this for a living and call themselves "freelancers."

And that was all it took. I was presented with an opportunity and several hours of digging later, I started my freelance career. Five-and-a-half years later, I am still going strong: I am fully self-employed, have a full freelance schedule, steady projects, and well-paying clients, all while having graduated from college less than four months ago.

So let me go back to the surfing, hunting, and digging that got me into this crazy world known as freelancing. Five years ago, I was hard-pressed to find ANY information about freelancing as a student. Sure, there was tons of

I had a very hard time finding any information on freelancing as a student.

information about freelancing on the side while keeping your full-time job, quitting your job to start freelancing, or turn a stay-at-home career into a stay-at-home career with a steady paycheck. But why not any information about freelancing part-time while going to college? Surely someone has done that before, right?

"Well maybe not," I thought to myself, especially after seeing so many posts and articles online with statements such as "you're not experienced enough to start freelancing in school," or the infamous, "you have to get a real job first after you graduate." But why?

To make a long, five-year story short, I ignored all of those nay-sayers and I am so glad I did. I read every book, website, article, and forum I could get my hungry little hands on. I took my very limited business knowledge (at the time) and

started working my ass off; learning new skills, working on getting clients, and working on making the freelance projects I did have awesome and the clients satisfied with my work and happy.

I tried and experimented with many different techniques when I started freelancing, especially when it came to getting clients, what to charge, how to keep the records, proposal techniques, etc. I tried all of these techniques but most of them failed mainly because those techniques I read about were directed to other types of freelancers, not student freelancers.

Over time, however, I started learning what worked for me and what would work given my student status. Lots of trial and error, lots of reading and thinking, and lots of trying and lets see-ing, I finally was able to gain control over this beast called freelancing and have it play well in the sandbox with my collegiate career.

Five long years later, I'm now a fresh graduate from college. I have a business growing faster than I can keep up with and I can confidently say that I won't be one of the graduates hunting for a regular 9-to-5 and work for "the man." All of this freelance success happened while I was a more-than-full-time college student, working hard toward two different degrees simultaneously, and had a part-time job for some of that time too. I wanted to prove the nay-sayers wrong. And I did (and still do).

I knew I was not alone. I knew there are students just like me who are interested in bucking the trend and joining the ranks of thousands upon thousands of self-employed individuals who call themselves freelancers. Like I said earlier, while there was virtually no information out there for students wanting to freelance, I wanted to change that, and I did when I launched *Students That Freelance* over my spring break in March 2010.

About This Handbook

While posting content about various topics in student freelancing is great for the *Students That Freelance* blog, it isn't comprehensive for those wanting to start freelancing as a student. That is where this book comes into play. More like a course, if you will, I worked to make this handbook a "pick up and run" type of book.

We are busy students with enough textbooks to read. We need something that will help us get the information we need and fast. We need a structure and a way to plan for an amazing journey into freelancing. What better way than structuring such a book similar to something we already know very well? So, this book is designed like a college course, minus all of the tons of reading, long term papers, and massive exams that we all dread.

I wrote and developed this book as a means to help you learn, plan, and start your own freelance career while still in school. I wrote it for the busy student taking six classes with tons of homework, for the student who participates in athletics that involve a rigorous schedule, and for the student who has a full course load and works a part-time or full-time job. I especially wrote it for the student who wants to make their own career path, earn a decent income, and who wants to work less for that income—all before they walk across that stage.

I couldn't agree more with one of my favorite music artists, Drake, who in one of his songs says, "I could relate to kids going straight to the league, when they recognize that you got what it takes to succeed.[1]" If you feel like you have what it takes to reach for something you want, then why wait until the rest of the world says you're ready?

I hope this book helps take you "straight to the league" and you become extremely successful in your career, all before you graduate and receive that well-earned diploma!

[1] Drake. "Thank Me Now." Thank Me Later. 2010. Cash Money Records, Universal Records, and UMG Recordings.

Lesson 1

Is Student Freelancing For You?

You've recently discovered the fascinating world of freelancing and are eager to learn more about it. You've heard so many great things about how you can earn some money in your free time and do what you love without it interfering with your school life or personal life. This idea has intrigued you enough to start doing research on your own. But, is it the right thing for you? Do you know all of what it takes to start freelancing? Is freelancing the only answer?

This lesson is designed to help you learn more about freelancing in general, what it takes to start freelancing, how it impacts your school career, and overall get you thinking about freelancing as a career. All of the things covered in this lesson will help you determine if freelancing as a student is the right decision for you.

1.1 Lecture What Is Student Freelancing?

The term "freelancing" can be used for many different things and is often defined in many different ways, but what does it mean in this book?

I'm glad you asked! In a nutshell, the term "freelancing" means *being an independent contractor who offers a service at a price.* While there are tons of books with different definitions, this is the boiled-down version.

When you start freelancing, you are considered an "independent contractor" in the eyes of the government (in the United States) and in the eyes of many large companies. This varies from being an employee in many ways including: you work for yourself and not one specific agency or company; instead of your employer paying the government taxes and taking some out of your check as well, you now pay both sides of the taxes from your income; and you have the entire world in which to conduct business where often employees are limited to who the company wants them to work with.

In other words, as a freelancer (or self-employed), you are both the employer and the employee. You handle all of the aspects of your employment—things that employers normally do like handling income and all of the things the employee does like actually doing the work. You are your own boss and you do all the work in your business. You set the rules and you follow the rules. Make sense?

Of course in other countries, the government may define an "employee" and an "independent contractor" differently than they do in the United States, but since I am in the U.S. and my experience is based on the law of the land here, this book will be based on U.S. laws.

However, there are many other self-employed individuals who do those things and are generally not called "freelancers." Why is that? Freelancers are most often associated with producing some sort of service (for the most part) for a short period of time, such as working on just one project for a client instead of working on everything only one client has (like an employer).

Freelancers are usually your graphic designers, web designers, consultants, photographers, music and/or video editors, copywriters, translators, event planners, web developers, writers, illustrators, virtual assistants, SEO specialists, etc. who meet the criteria above.

The word "free" in freelancing doesn't mean you can't charge for the services you offer or that people expect you to do it for free (although most of them wish you would). All of the types of freelancers I just mentioned offer their services for a fee, such as photographers charging per wedding or per hour to take photographs. The "free" part of freelancing simply means you are independent and you work for yourself.

The most important thing to keep in mind: you are your own boss. You control what you work on, what services you provide, who you work with, and what you charge. That is what makes you "independent." You don't have two bosses over you at all times dictating what you do. You have a client in which you partner with to create a mutually-beneficial relationship where an exchange occurs (often you provide a service such as web design or copywriting, and they pay you for it).

1.2 Quiz Are You Prepared to Be a Student Freelancer?

Freelancing as a student isn't right for everyone. The following quiz will see if you are ready!

Think you have what it takes to succeed as a student freelancer? With the pressures of doing well in school, getting homework done, and finding a way to pay the bills, can you stay motivated and keep up with what is surely to be a hectic schedule? The following is a quiz to see how well adapted you are to becoming a successful student freelancer, and what you may still need to work on.

DIRECTIONS: On a scale from 1 to 5, with 1 being strongly disagree and 5 being strongly agree, rate the following questions and/or statements based on the skills and abilities you have now. This quiz will help you prepare for other lessons in this book so honesty counts!

_____ 1.) Are you naturally a very organized person?

_____ 2.) Are you able to make a plan of action to get something done, and stick to that plan?

_____ 3.) Do you feel as though you manage and budget your money well?

(continued on the next page)

_____ 4.) Can you make your own schedule and keep to it?

_____ 5.) You feel comfortable asking (sometimes repeatedly) for money that is owed to you.

_____ 6.) Do you manage your time well so you don't procrastinate with looming deadlines?

_____ 7.) You can recognize when you don't know something and you work to find ways to learn about them.

_____ 8.) Do you normally keep detailed records of important things, such as your bank accounts and spending habits?

_____ 9.) You see yourself as a self-motivator and can motivate yourself to get up and get moving on a growing to do list.

_____ 10.) Are your taxes normally very organized when April comes around (you aren't pulling together receipts on April 13th)?

_____ 11.) Do you like taking on a challenge?

_____ 12.) Are you a fast learner?

_____ 13.) You see yourself as a confident person, especially around people you haven't met before.

_____ 14.) Do you communicate well with others?

_____ 15.) Do you see yourself as a hard worker, willing to do anything (legal) to get the job done to the best of your ability?

_____ 16.) You can handle rejection and/or criticism very well and learn from them.

_____ 17.) Do you keep calm when deadlines are quickly approaching and stress is building?

_____ 18.) You are a natural born leader with a take charge attitude and people admire that about you.

_____ 19.) You are not afraid to work long hours to get something done.

_____ 20.) Do you see freelancing as a long term career, not something that you do only while in school?

Add up all twenty scores from the quiz to determine your score out of a possible 100: _____

While it seems like a lot of these questions are pretty generic-sounding, there are tons of situations as a student freelancer where the qualities discussed are needed. So how well did you do?

SCORING: Take your final score and look below to see which range your score falls. Read the statement that corresponds with that range to see how well equipped you are to start freelancing as a student.

81-100: You're born to be a student freelancer and have what it takes to do big things! What are you waiting for?

61-80: You're lacking a few of the qualities of a student freelancer, but you are eager and willing to develop them to become successful.

41-60: You have the drive, but are lacking some of the gear. It will take hard work and determination to sharpen the qualities it takes to be a successful student freelancer, but not completely impossible.

21-40: You lack confidence and many qualities of a successful student freelancer, but hey, Rome wasn't built in a day, was it?

0-20: While you love the idea of freelancing while in school, maybe now isn't the best time to take the leap. Checkout lesson 1.8 to find ways to build your skills and confidence to try freelancing later.

1.3 Exercise Why Do You Want to Freelance as a Student?

Everyone starts freelancing for different reasons, but what is your reason(s) to start freelancing while still in school? Let's uncover some of those reasons.

No matter what got you thinking about starting a freelance career in the first place, the reason(s) behind doing things such as researching about freelancing and even buying this book are ones we want to keep in mind. Our reasoning behind things change frequently and become deeply rooted in most of the decisions we make. In this exercise we are going to discuss the reasons and deeper motivations for becoming a student freelancer.

Why?

Why do I want you to consider the deeper reasons and motivations for freelancing as a student? Often these reasons will help keep you motivated and driven when the going gets tough. If you think you are going to do it for a source of extra money right now, then when there is no extra money flowing in for a while, you could be more willing to seek a steady part-time job and stop freelancing. On the other hand, if your reasons included wanting to start your own business, you probably would be more inclined to push through the rough times and stick with it.

To put it another way, these act as your motivations. Having deep-seeded reasons why you want to start freelancing will help you get through any tough times you may have as a student freelancer.

DIRECTIONS: More of a deep thinking exercise, think of all the reasons why you want to start freelancing. As you work through the reasons, write them down using the lines below and think about why those are reasons. You will often find that there are deeper reasons behind your desire to become a freelancer while still in school.

For example, maybe you want to start freelancing as a way to gain experience in the industry. That's great! But what if you end up not getting any projects and that experience isn't happening like you originally thought? What will keep you motivated to continue freelancing, or is that your sign that maybe you should do something else to gain industry experience?

Go ahead and give it a go. Write down your reasons for freelancing in the lines below. You may want to think about the reasons for the next several days to make sure you have uncovered all of them.

_____

_____

_____

_____

_____

_____

_____

1.4 Lecture Benefits and Drawbacks as a Student Freelancer

While freelancing as a student has numerous perks, it comes with its fair share of drawbacks as well, all of which are important to know.

Freelancing while still in school has numerous benefits, many of which are the reasons why more and more students are starting to freelance while in school. Who could blame them? I'm sure some of those reasons are the same reasons that led you to start investigating freelancing as a student (and led you to buy this book).

One of the biggest benefits of student freelancing is it gives you a jump start on your career. This is often the case with students who are going to school in the same field they want to start freelancing in. Most often, students want

> *One of the biggest benefits of freelancing as a student is to get a jump start on your career.*

to start gaining industry experience as soon as possible, and freelancing is a great way for them to be able to.

With industry experience comes business experience and professionalism. Both are things we will discuss later, but

when you freelance you are not only a great photographer or writer, you are also the owner, manager, accountant, marketer, customer service rep, and every one else in your business. These are skills that are vital to any self-employed person's success.

Another big benefit is income potential. While freelancing doesn't bring in big bucks overnight, it does give students the potential to earn more money with (typically) less time involved. I'm not saying that you will get to pull in a full-time income working only two hours a week, but you could earn more per hour for the hours you do work.

While the benefits listed above are the big benefits of freelancing as a student, there are several others as well, such as:

- Getting student discounts on equipment and supplies for your business.
- Getting a leg-up where it comes to finding a job compared to your classmates (if you plan to find a full-time job after you graduate).

- Developing a real-world portfolio instead of a portfolio 100% dependent on school projects.
- Building your reputation in the industry way before most of your classmates.

The biggest drawback for freelancing as a student is having no industry experience. Kind of a catch-22, huh? The biggest benefit of student freelancing is to gain experience, but the fact you have no industry experience (or very little) to start with is a huge disadvantage when it comes to seeking projects and working with clients. This is one of the reasons why students are becoming more and more attracted to options such as freelancing because they can get a head start on gaining such experience in their own way.

While most other freelancers have years of experience working for someone else before they start freelancing, chances are you don't. This can hurt you if you are not a fast learner and eager to learn the ropes quick.

Being taken advantage of is another huge drawback. Since you're a student, most people equate your student status with being less-experienced and you offering work on the cheap. You don't have to be any of those things! You will have to learn how to get around this drawback when clients want to take advantage of your time, price, or your work.

Other drawbacks include:

- Less and less time available to do everything you want to do because you are spending more of your time freelancing and trying to keep up with classes.
- You often have to work to gain clients when you aren't making money. In other words, you often have to work for your freelance business knowing that you aren't making money until you have client projects on deck.
- Getting clients can be even more difficult than it is for a typical freelancer since your network is fairly small and your student status may deter prospects.
- Not knowing much about legal or business aspects may slow you down or worse—make you more liable when you make mistakes that could negatively affect your business.
- You'll find yourself not knowing everything you need to know in your industry, which can be a cause of discouragement and stress.

It's important to remember to keep these drawbacks in mind but don't let them hold you back! With time, experience, and education, these drawbacks will become less and less hindering as you progress through your freelancing career. Also, many of the drawbacks listed above I will cover throughout this book.

1.5 Exercise Exploring Fields of Freelancing

From photographers, designers, and web developers, to artists, accountants, and personal shoppers; the different fields of freelancing that students can pursue are staggering.

While you're thinking about starting your freelancing career as a student, what field most accurately describes the type of freelancing you want to pursue? You may already know that you want to be a photographer or game designer, but have you taken time to research what all is required, or better yet, are there other freelancers already doing what you want to do?

This exercise will help you start thinking about what field you are wanting to pursue in your freelancing and what you enjoy doing most in that field. For example, if you want to be a photographer, what type of photographs do you want to take (i.e. portraits, events, art, nature, weddings)? Are there others freelancing in that field of freelancing as well?

DIRECTIONS: Brainstorm what exactly you want to do as a freelancer, then research to see if there are others who are currently freelancing in that same field. If you happen to run across something that is required in that field such as any computer software, specific gear such as cameras, or maybe special licensure, write that down too, as that could be valuable later down the road. Fill in the blanks on this page and the next page to help keep your thoughts organized in one place.

What field of freelancing most accurately describes the type of freelancing you want to pursue?

Desired field(s) of freelancing (photography, event planning, web design, etc.):

_____

_____

_____

What type of freelancing in that field(s)? (family portraits, weddings, website design e-commerce, etc.):

_____

_____

_____

(continued on the next page)

Are there others out there doing what you want to do? If so write down their names and/or websites below:

_____

_____

_____

_____

Did you happen to run across any juicy information about the field of freelancing you're wanting to pursue, such as common characteristics, software used, most provided service, necessary equipment, etc.?

_____

_____

_____

_____

Financial Expectations as a Student Freelancer.

I'm sure by now you are wondering how much you can expect to make as a freelancer in the field you just researched about, and it is a good thing to start thinking about. One very quick way to find out what you can expect to make in a particular field is to do a quick Google search for "freelance industry report." You may find links to reports on the International Freelancer's Day website, to the book "Freelance Confidential" by Amanda Hackwith, or even articles written about the current state of the freelance industry. All of these are great resources to see what the average freelancer in your field of freelancing makes. Remember to keep in mind though that most freelancers are doing this full-time, so since you are probably going to be doing it about one-third to one-half of the time they are, it is best to divide those numbers accordingly. This is just to give you a rough idea; we'll talk more later in the book about how to price your services based on what you want to make.

Students who currently work to pay their bills are in a completely different situation than those who don't currently work or have bills. With each situation different from the next, it is important to figure out the best way to start your freelancing career as a student.

We all have different situations where it comes to school, family, work, church, friends, sports, etc. Should you go all in and make freelancing your sole source of income or keep your part-time job while you start? With all of us having a special and unique combination of the above, there is no "one size fits all" solution when it comes to starting a freelancing career as a student.

There is, however, a right and wrong way to start freelancing given your specific situation. For instance, it isn't a good idea to quit your job to pursue freelancing full-time for the first time when you need to pay bills such as rent or car payments. However, for the student who already has a financial backing either by their parents, spouse, or student loans, freelancing could be a great opportunity to start earning an income and gain industry experience right away.

DIRECTIONS: On the next two pages are different scenarios that most students may fall in. Review the following and determine which one most closely matches your current situation, then go over the suggestions on how you should start freelancing as a student.

Scenario 1

You are a full-time student, but don't work a part-time job for income. You have some spare time but don't want to get a job in fear of losing your open schedule. Most of your expenses are paid by student loans, your parents, or your spouse, so money earned is for things you want.

SUGGESTION: Go all in! You don't have anything to lose as you will still be financially secure for when times are not so fruitful. While freelancing may take away some of your spare time, it still gives you flexibility to allow you to do things you want to do.

Scenario 2

You go to school part-time or full-time but have a very serious job. It's serious because it pays for everything you need: school, books, food, car and transportation, and your dorm or apartment.

SUGGESTION: If you have any spare time, start with a few freelance projects here and there while keeping your job and before giving your boss your two-weeks' notice. Save up money and when you have enough savings and experience, jump all the way in!

Scenario 3

You are a full-time student with a part-time job and still live at home or in a dorm/apartment where your parents are paying for most of your expenses. You work at a part-time job mainly to have spending money for fun stuff like concerts, new clothes, or to go to parties.

SUGGESTION: You could go either way, either quit your job and start freelancing right away, or keep your job but take on a freelance project from time to time to get your toes wet. With this situation, you can ease into freelancing to test the waters.

1.7 Exercise Priorities - Time and School Impact

Freelancing while going to school means you are adding an additional activity to your already slammed schedule, which could potentially take time away from other, more important things.

While it often doesn't seem like work, freelancing can and does limit your time you could (and maybe should) be spending doing other things like homework, spending time with family and friends, and doing things you enjoy such as exercising and playing games.

Freelancing gives you a lot of flexibility when it comes to when you actually "work," but your current responsibilities, obligations, and priorities may not allow for it. You also don't want your freelancing to cause negative effects when it comes to your schooling, such as

Freelancing gives you a lot of flexibility when it comes to when you actually "work."

not having time to adequately do your homework or study for tests to keep your grades up.

In this exercise, we are going to examine your schedule and priorities to see if and how much time you can devote to freelancing while being a student. Some math is involved, but don't worry—it's easy.

DIRECTIONS: Prioritize the following activities (and add ones or scratch through those that don't apply to you as necessary) starting with writing the number 1 next to the most important priority (in the blank on the left), then with a number 2 for the next, and so on and so forth. Then realistically figure out how many hours a week each of the activities require, including time getting ready to leave (shower, getting dressed, getting your things together, etc.) and the amount of travel time it takes you to get there and back (if you have to leave the house) and write that number in the second blank.

_____ School   _____ hours

_____ Studying   _____ hours

_____ Current Job(s)   _____ hours

_____ Church   _____ hours

_____ Family Time   _____ hours

_____ Spending Time with Friends   _____ hours

_____ Athletics   _____ hours

_____ Organizations   _____ hours

_____ (Other) _____ _____ hours

_____ (Other) _____ _____ hours

_____ (Other) _____ _____ hours

_____ (Other) _____ _____ hours

_____ (Other) _____ _____ hours

Total up how many hours you listed above: _____ hours. This is how many hours you spend doing things you are currently obligated to or responsible for.

Next, we need to figure out if you have any free time for freelancing, given your current obligations and responsibilities. What other things do you do on the daily or weekly basis that consumes large portions of your time? I can think of at least three: sleeping, chores (laundry, grocery shopping, cooking dinner, etc), and general relaxation or down time.

DIRECTIONS: Figure up the hours you spend doing things other than the activities listed on the previous page, such as sleep and chores, and realistically estimate how long you spend doing each every week. There are some blank lines to add additional things if necessary.

Sleep   _____ hours

Chores   _____ hours

Relaxation or down time   _____ hours

(Other) _____   _____ hours

(Other) _____   _____ hours

(Other) _____   _____ hours

(Other) _____   _____ hours

(Other) _____   _____ hours

Total up these hours: _____ hours.

Now add the total from your obligations and responsibilities from the previous page with the total above to come up with total hours spent: _____ hours.

Hopefully the number of hours you spend doing things is less than 168 hours, or the number of hours you have in a week (7 days). Subtract the number above from 168 to get your total "free" hours: _____ free hours.

Now, do you have more than fifteen free hours a week to dedicate to all things freelancing, such as projects, marketing, getting new clients, and basic administrative work such as billing and phone calls?

If so, then you are in a great position to start freelancing with your current schedule (if you don't let go of any activities listed earlier or quit any jobs you have).

If not, are you willing to give up a low-priority activity (remember when you prioritized the activities by number?) in order to start freelancing? For instance, are you willing to quit your job or reduce the amount of down time you get?

Now that you have your priorities and an idea of how you spend your time, take some time (no pun intended) to figure out if you really do want to take on another activity that will consume a significant chunk of your time. If you still aren't sure, then maybe it is worth waiting until your schedule frees up some before you start freelancing.

1.8 Lecture Not Quite Ready to Start Freelancing as a Student?

After reading through this lesson and learning all of the things involved in freelancing, are you prepared for the challenges that lay ahead?

For some of you, maybe you are beginning to think freelancing isn't quite for you, or maybe you aren't fully ready to join the ranks of thousands of freelancers. There is no shame in that. So in what ways can you work to become better prepared and ready for starting your career a student freelancer?

Internships are a great place to look. Look to see if there is a program at school that supports internships and start working with your internship coordinator to find a great

If you aren't quite ready to start freelancing, you can look into options such as internships, a part-time job in your industry, or even form a collaborative with fellow students.

internship. Even if your school doesn't support internships, it never hurts to try and find an internship that can help you start gaining experience. The benefit with internships is that they often provide an avenue to start building your network.

Related to finding an internship is finding a part-time job in your field. Working at a part-time job in your field for a year or so will help you gain experience and confidence to start freelancing on your own. Most firms are willing to hire students part-time so they can learn how the industry works. This is invaluable experience that could definitely be beneficial to your future freelancing success.

Or maybe you are ready to start freelancing, but don't feel like you are ready to do it on your own. Students partner up all the time to form collaboratives and work together to achieve their goals. Have a friend who wants to start their own business, but don't know what kind of business? Maybe you can partner with them with your culinary skills to open a bakery. Know of great web designer at your school that needs your amazing web development skills? The possibilities are endless and can help all of you in more ways than one.

Since I gave you a brief run down on what to expect as a student freelancer, are you really ready to start your freelancing endeavors?

As a way to help sum up this lesson (and every other lesson in this book), it's time to test you on what you have learned! I have discussed what freelancing is, different fields of freelancing, and how everyone's situation is different. You have quizzed yourself to see if you are ready, wrote down why you wanted to start freelancing, got your priorities in line and figured out if you have time to start freelancing.

DIRECTIONS: Are you ready to start freelancing? Below is a list of statements pulled from the different topics in this lesson. Answer each with "true" or "false" based on your knowledge gained in this lesson.

TRUE   FALSE

T   **F**   1.) Sources such as freelance industry reports can give a starting student freelancer a good idea of how much they could make as a freelancer in their particular field of freelancing.

T   **F**   2.) Being a freelancer means that you work for someone else and have no say in the type of work you do.

T   **F**   3.) Every student freelancer's situation is exactly the same, so what works for one student freelancer will work for all student freelancers.

T   **F**   4.) It's safe to say a student can start freelancing if they determine they have a minimum of fifteen free hours a week to work on client projects, marketing, and general administration

T   **F**   5.) A drawback of freelancing as a student is it could hinder your ability to gain industry experience.

T **F**   6.) Qualities of student freelancers include being a leader, self-motivator, organized, and a fast learner.

T **F**   7.) If you start to feel like freelancing is not the best thing for you to pursue while being a student, you should try anyways.

T **F**   8.) Difficulty in finding and gaining clients is a drawback to starting a freelance career while being a student.

T **F**   9.) For students who start a career as a freelancer, the reasons behind doing so are often pretty simple which make the decision to start freelancing an easy one.

T **F**   10.) If you live on your own and must work in order to pay the bills and eat, it is not a good idea to quit your existing job and start freelancing the next day.

SCORING: Check your answers circled above with the ones below to see how much you have learned. If you missed one, now is a great time to review what you missed to make sure your knowledge about freelancing is rock-solid moving forward. Each answer below is followed with the corresponding lesson.

1.) **TRUE.** While determining what field of freelancing you would like to pursue, coming to an understanding of the respective financial expectations should be required research. Along with deciding on your field of freelancing, we also discussed looking in freelancing industry reports to find out what other freelancers are making. Keep in mind though that most freelancers surveyed in those reports work full-time, and as a student you are less likely to work the same hours they do. *LESSON 1.5*

2.) **FALSE.** When you start your career as a freelancer, be it student or not, you become self-employed, meaning that you work for yourself. You have no boss; you are your own boss. You can determine what you want to work on, when you want to work, and with who you want to work with. You have all the say in your business and your job, which is an amazing feeling! *LESSON 1.1*

3.) **FALSE.** I dedicated an entire section on why every single student freelancer has a different situation. For instance, there are students that live at home with their parents and work to have money for clothes and fun events while there are students that live on their own and have bills they have to pay every month. The big theme throughout this book is that no two student freelancers are alike, so what works for one student may not work for another. *LESSON 1.6*

4.) **TRUE.** We talked about priorities and how starting your freelancing career could impact your time for school and your personal life. When determining how much time you need to take on such an endeavor, we stated that having roughly fifteen hours a week or more to dedicate to client work, invoicing, marketing, and other essential tasks relating to freelancing would be ideal when starting a business while still in school. *LESSON 1.7*

5.) **FALSE.** It is a benefit of student freelancing that you can start gaining industry experience earlier than your classmates. Gaining this experience earlier and expanding it quicker than your fellow classmates can only lead to more and better opportunities in your future career no matter if you choose to continue freelancing or seek full-time employment. *LESSON 1.4*

6.) **TRUE.** Remember taking the quiz to determine if you are prepared for the crazy but great life of a student freelancer? These are all qualities that many student freelancers share, including other qualities such as being

able to budget money well, manage your time well, keeping detailed records, and enjoy taking on challenges. *LESSON 1.2*

7.) **FALSE.** While freelancing has its benefits such as expanding your experience, there are other ways to achieve the same benefits and/or prepare yourself for a self-employed career. If you aren't ready to freelance now, don't force yourself to. Look for other opportunities such as internships and part-time jobs in your particular field to gain experience and confidence, then reevaluate becoming a freelancer. These types of opportunities may even be able to help you be a better freelancer should you decide to start freelancing later. *LESSON 1.8*

8.) **TRUE.** It could be a bit more difficult to find clients as a student freelancer due to factors such as your student status, experience, and a small network to work from. Clients often see that being a student means you are inexperienced and it could make it even harder to land them as a client. *LESSON 1.4*

9.) **FALSE.** It is often not advised to make the decision to freelance overnight, no matter if you are a student or not. There are often much deeper reasons that need to be analyzed in order to make the decision to start freelancing and keep you motivated and focused through often tough times. *LESSON 1.3*

10.) **TRUE.** Every student's situation is different, which means how they start freelancing will be different too. We went through three scenarios that cover most student freelancers' situations, one of which was if you have a job that you depend on to pay for everything from your tuition to your rent, then you should keep your job and slowly build your freelancing business on the side until you feel confident enough in your freelancing income to say good-bye to your job. *LESSON 1.6*

GRADE: No one is keeping track of your grades, however if you would like to grade yourself, below is the easy formula to calculate how well you did!

How many you got right: _____ Divided by 10 = _____ x 100 = _____ %

Example: Answered 8 right. 8 / 10 = .8 x 100 = 80%

What's coming up next?
In the next lesson, I'm going to talk about creating a plan that will start your freelancing career. Everything from getting all of your ideas down on paper, organizing them to creating a business plan, researching the industry, and finding a mentor will be discussed. Keep in mind your freelancing success is only as good as the plan and foundation that you build it on. I'll see you in the next lesson!

Lesson 2

Creating the Blueprint

While it would be easy to just jump right into making your website, determining your services, and answering the question "how much should I charge," we have to start things off on the right foot. If you want to be successful, you should start with a solid foundation and a plan to boot.

This lesson is all about laying the foundation to the start of your freelancing success. In other words, this is all the things that freelancers who fell into freelancing wish they did before they got started. We will go over things like writing down your ideas, researching the industry, finding a mentor, and developing a financial safety net. Consider this lesson as the way to create your blueprint to your freelancing success as a student!

2.1 Lecture Looking at the Big Picture

Thinking about and starting to plan your student freelancing career is very similar to building a house. Starting with a strong foundation will keep things straight.

I'm sure you have heard of the "building a house" metaphor before: you start with the foundation, build the structure, then bring it all together with a roof, and finishing with the final details. It's true that it can be applied to just about anything. Without being too cliché and possibly borderline corny, thinking about building your freelancing career as a student has all of the same elements as you would have when building a house.

I'm not going to sit here and explain what part of freelancing is the foundation, which part is the roof, and so on, because I'm positive you are smart and know what I am about to say anyways, so I will spare you the corny references.

Instead, I'm going talk about starting the process of thinking and actually planning out your freelancing career while going to school. As you may already know, it is one thing to have all of these thoughts and ideas and most importantly excitement about starting your freelance career, it is quite another to get a plan made out and start following it to make those ideas come to life.

It's awesome that you have tons of ideas and are super excited to start this freelancing journey, and I want you to keep thinking of amazing ideas and stay excited. However, in order to make all of those ideas a reality and start living that excitement day in and day out, a solid plan and framework needs to be developed and put into place to ensure your success as a student freelancer.

Don't worry. Throughout this lesson I am going to help you do just that: get all of your thoughts and ideas out there,

Developing a plan before you begin freelancing can help you stay focused and achieve your goals much sooner.

develop a plan, and make sure your plan is ready to be put into place. The most important thing to keep in mind while you work through this lesson is to really give it everything you've got. Your plan will only be as good as you make it. Spend time on creating a plan. Take the time to go through this chapter slowly, and repeatedly if necessary.

2.2 Quiz **Have You Thought About These Things Yet?**

Your mind is full of ideas and you are excited to get started, but have you thought about these things yet?

While we all feel like we are prepared for the challenges that freelancing is sure to present, we may forget to think about some minor details in our road to becoming successful self-employed individuals. Most of you who are reading this book probably don't have much in the way of experience dealing with the business end of a small business. I am also (almost) certain that most of you have never started a business either.

Being a self-employed newbie has its perks. For instance, your mind is full of exciting ideas, you're focused and motivated to achieve something great, and you have time available to dedicate to a business idea. However, not being through the ropes of starting a business before has its drawbacks as well, such as not knowing important laws relating to your business, little to no experience with self-employment taxes, and not knowing what to plan for.

Scary right? It doesn't have to be! To give you a heads up, this section is about seeing what you have thought about and what you haven't when it comes to starting your freelancing career as a student. Don't get stressed out either! Many of the topics in the quiz below are covered throughout this book.

DIRECTIONS: Read through the following questions and honestly ask yourself if you know and have thought about these different subject areas. I've provided some lines for you to write down what you have thought about or to help guide you in things you haven't. There are no wrong or right answers, however, answering them honestly can help you down the road.

1.) Have you thought about all of the taxes you may be responsible for not only at the federal level, but state, county, and city level as well?

_____

_____

(continued on the next page)

2.) Do you know that planning out a business is just as important than actually starting and running a business?

_____

_____

3.) What types of marketing are you planning to use? Your clients have to find you some how!

_____

_____

4.) Think you may need to take out insurance on your business? If so, what kind of insurance and how much? If not, do you know who you can talk to about your insurance needs?

_____

_____

5.) Have you started thinking about how you are going to manage your money, not only the money that your business makes but your personal money as well?

_____

_____

Like I said, there is no right or wrong answers to the above, but hopefully this will help get your mind thinking about all the little things required for your freelancing as a student as you progress through this book.

If you haven't already noticed, many of the topics above that will be discussed throughout this book has nothing to do with the field of freelancing you are going in to. Crazy right? This is because while most freelancers are extremely talented designers, developers, illustrators, writers, and the like, most of them lack that same skill level when it comes to the business end of things.

2.3 Exercise Getting Your Ideas on Paper

Keeping track of your ideas and things to do can help put your mind at ease and allows you to always reference them later on.

I fell into freelancing, so most of my ideas didn't come until later. However, I am sure that so far you have tons of ideas about your freelancing, ranging from how to start, to what services to offer, to all the awesome marketing techniques you can use. Most freelancers start their freelancing careers with just that: tons of ideas that they can't wait to put into action when they start freelancing.

Ideas not only create excitement but can help you set goals to achieve and keep you motivated. However, just like anything you think about, if you don't take time to write down or sketch out your ideas, they could flee.

Some of the ideas you may be having include business names, how you would set up your schedule, what things you want to learn, what type of clients you want to work with, and maybe even down to the colors you want in your logo and how you want your website to look. No idea is too small, silly, out-of-place, or wrong.

For example, you may want to integrate your love for photography and web design, or know of a really neat marketing technique that you can't wait to try out. These are the great ideas I'm taking about and the ones you can use not only throughout this book, but later in your freelancing career to help boost your success.

In this exercise, we are going to take all of those ideas that are bouncing around in your mind and get them down on paper. We don't want those ideas to be lost forever, as they could help you in your freelancing career later on.

DIRECTIONS: Take several days to not only write down those ideas you currently have, but brainstorm for any other ideas you may have about starting your freelancing career as a student. Write out all the details you can think of in the lines on the next page and be as specific as possible.

Write all your ideas here!

_____
_____
_____
_____
_____
_____
_____
_____
_____
_____
_____
_____
_____
_____
_____
_____
_____
_____

Reading Freelancing Books and Websites To Generate More Ideas.

When I decided to relaunch my freelancing business recently, I had all kinds of ideas in my mind, but once I started writing them down and getting them out of my head, I felt like I didn't have enough ideas. Are you feeling the same way? There are tons of ways to generate new ideas. One of my favorite ways is to read other freelancing books, websites, and blogs to see what other freelancers are saying. This helps me generate ideas quickly. Often these sites are designed to help other freelancers, so if it can help you generate ideas that you could later put to use, then why not take advantage of them and write them down?

2.4 Exercise Researching The Industry

Any business book will tell you: research the industry! But how can that be applied to the field of freelancing you are going to, especially as a student freelancer?

"Research the industry!" Sounds simple enough, but what does it really mean? Before I break down the "what," let me cover the "why" first.

I see it quite often; many freelancers start without really taking time to understand the industry or field they are going into. I don't mean they don't understand how to operate Photoshop to make killer photographs or can code in HTML and CSS to make the next best website. What I mean is that most freelancers, especially students, lack the knowledge and experience that goes along with "being in the industry."

I dedicate an entire section in this book to researching the industry for various reasons, the main one is to help you understand the reality that is present-day freelancing. Most freelancers have done extremely well for themselves and have never done any research on their industry, but they worked extremely hard to get there. Taking the adequate time to research the industry can help you take that leap forward in many aspects of your freelancing, including an estimate of how

much to charge, what the working environment is like for freelancers (and if that is something you want to be apart of or stray from), give you a boost of confidence, and inform you if your field of freelancing is "popular" or not (using the term "popular" loosely).

Now that I've covered "why" you want to research the industry, let's talk about "what" you will want to research. While there are many different types of freelancers reading

> Researching the industry allows you to collect a lot of information and provide a reality check.

this book, I'm going to cover various ways to do research that span most fields of freelancing. Some may apply to you, but others may not.

With that said, the main things you want to find out about your industry or anything relating to your freelancing as a student includes the who, what, when, where, and how questions. For example "what do others charge," "when do they typically work," and "how do they find clients."

One huge resource that I wish I had paid more attention to six years ago (2007) when I started freelancing as a student are the various freelance industry reports that are published pretty much yearly. While there are many flavors of reports published now, I don't recall too many being developed and published when I started.

For 2012, there are two main freelance-focused industry reports that are fairly large in scale and cover quite a bit of topics relating to freelancing and self-employment fields.

Industry reports can give you an idea of specific elements of freelancing, such as the average rate for your experience.

Although these are not industry-specific (such as only for web developers or only for photographers), they do feature information and statistics for many different fields of freelancing.

Those two large freelance industry reports include the "2011 Freelance Industry Report" published by International Freelancers Day and the survey done by FreelanceSwitch which was analyzed and published in book format for purchase called "Freelance Confidential: The Whole Truth on Successful Freelancing" by Amanda Hackwith (links to both are in the sidebar on the next page).

Both of these resources have information that can drastically change the way you think about freelancing and the way you approach your own freelancing. For example, both of these reports feature statistics about income based on experience and the type of freelancer they are (i.e. web designer, writer, photographer, etc.). Why would this be valuable for you? It can give you an idea of how much other freelancers are earning for the work they do, how much you could charge (divide the average by billable hours), and if it is a profitable field .

Another great statistic they both have is average age of a freelancer and education level. As a student freelancer, these are figures that interest me the most. For instance one of them lists 14% of freelancers are between 20-29 years old (2011 Freelance Industry Report), while the other is much more specific by giving age groups and their average hourly rate and annual income (21-30 year olds average roughly $49 dollars an hour according to "Freelance Confidential"). While we aren't being scientific here, it could be said that 14% of freelancers are in their 20's and make an average of $50 per hour. No wonder freelancing as a student is becoming more and more attractive!

While those are the two big reports relating to freelancing specifically, there are tons of other articles and resources online that you could use to get a better idea of your field of freelancing. Google is your best friend in this case. Places like Forbes, Wall Street Journal, Harvard Business Review, and the like all publish articles and studies from time to time relating to self-employment, freelancing, and small business in general.

Others may post articles about "up-and-coming" fields such as mobile app development and list many valid points as to why these are hot fields for freelancers and small start-ups. Just keep in mind that any article or study you find, check who is writing the article and the site that it is published on. Just like citing reputable sources for a class paper, make sure the information you're gathering and reading are from a well-known and reputable sources so that you are not steered in the wrong direction!

Researching your industry is not meant to be a daunting task, but is supposed to be a great source of information and inspiration to help guide you through the process of starting your own freelancing career as a student. These resources are meant to help give you some sort of

Freelancing Industry Reports.
As mentioned in this lesson, there are two main freelancing industry reports that have great information about what you can expect as a freelancer. The first being the "2011 Freelance Industry Report" published by International Freelancers Day, which can be found here as a free download: http://www. internationalfreelancersday.com/2011report/. The other is available through Rockable Press titled "Freelance Confidential: The Whole Truth on Successful Freelancing" by Amanda Hackwith. At the time of this writing, "Freelance Confidential" is available for $39.99 (paperback) or $29.00 (ebook) through this link: http:// rockablepress.com/books/freelance-confidential.

foundation and reference when you start planning out your freelancing such as developing a business plan, setting your hourly rate, and forming a marketing plan.

DIRECTIONS: Start looking up the two reports I mentioned and read through them for facts and information relating to you as a student freelancer and the field of freelancing you're wanting to enter. Look specifically for information relating to income, education, hours freelancers work, working conditions, where they get their clients, etc. Start Googling for articles relating to freelancing and your specific field of freelancing.

There is a plethora of information out there! Read through all the information you find and pick out the bits that you feel are the most useful when you start planning your freelancing career. Since there is tons of information, I have supplied several lines below to help you keep all the information in one place. Don't forget to put where you found that information from (just like a college paper, but no need to be as detailed!) so that you can go back later and read more should you feel you need more information.

2.5 Exercise Finding a Mentor

Everyone needs a helping hand, even when they start freelancing!

At the time, I didn't label them specifically as "mentors," but there were many others in the graphic design and web design world that I contacted and "picked their brains" when I was started freelancing. And I really needed help.

While you could probably start your freelancing with little to no help from others, it's always better to find someone who is willing to help show you the ropes and get you started. This can be pretty much anyone: another freelancer local to you, a professor who does freelance work as well, a friend or family member who owns and runs their own business, or anyone.

And hey, you are a student after all. You have access to tons and tons of resources right in front of you! For instance, my university has a small business development center (more specifically the "Tennessee Small Business Development Center" or "TSBDC" for short). I met with the director there twice, right on my university's campus, and received a tremendous amount of help where it came to the business end of things—specifically my business plan.

When you start finding people who you can talk to about your freelancing, start a conversation with them (which you will do in the following exercise). You don't have to be so detailed as to ask them "will you be my mentor?" but starting a sincere conversation will allow you to get some help you need without putting too much pressure on the person you are talking to (that often comes with being labeled a "mentor"). Just remember to be respectful of their time!

DIRECTIONS: With the amazing amount of resources you have at your fingertips being a student, start looking for people that can help you with your freelancing. You don't have to specifically label them a "mentor," but anyone you can find who are willing to help you with your

freelancing goals are a great resource! Make a list of people you can contact (using the lines below) and start a genuine conversation with them. Repeat this process until you can find at least one solid person (hopefully two) you can rely on to help you. Write their names and contact information in the lines below to help you stay organized.

_____

_____

_____

_____

_____

_____

_____

_____

Mentor #1: _____

Mentor #2: _____

Remember to thank your mentor!

Always, always, always go out of your way to thank whoever helps you with your freelancing business. Be it a professor, business owner, another freelancer, anyone: make sure to thank them sincerely for their help. They didn't have to help you at all, but did because they believe in you!

2.6 Lecture Financial Safety Net

First things first. Before you can even start planning your leap into freelancing as a student, you have to make sure you can pay the bills when you start freelancing.

For those students who want to make freelancing their only job, they need to have some moolah in the bank to cover them when times get tough and cash flow is low.

Any freelancer will tell you that you need to have a savings and emergency fund to draw from. Most freelancers have had times where they had to pull from their funds when they first started freelancing.

If you are dependent on your job to pay bills such as your car insurance or rent, then a savings and an emergency fund is crucial. It is recommended that you put back six months worth of expenses into an emergency fund. This is because when you start seeing times getting tough and need to figure out what to do to pay the bills, this gives you enough time to start finding another source of income while drawing from your emergency fund.

If you have financial support through other means (parents, spouse, or student loans), the amount of financial security to start with can be a little less. I would aim for around three months of your out-of-pocket expenses to put

back for an emergency if this situation applies to you (we discussed different students' situations in lesson 1.6).

Taking a hard look at your financial situation will help you make some decisions, such as exactly when you can start freelancing. However, the worst assumption you can make is to start thinking freelancing will bring in buckets of money the day you start, because it won't. You have to keep in mind that in freelancing there is no regular paycheck and there is a delay in when you do the work and when you actually get paid for it.

Having a financial safety net will help keep your stress level down as well, which in turn helps keep you healthy and motivated. When your stress level is high and you are worried about money (and on top of that you have no financial security), that compounds your stress. However, if it has been a few weeks and you haven't gotten paid, then that emergency savings will reduce your stress—that is until you get to a point where you can't replenish it before it runs dry.

2.7 Exercise Developing the Business Plan

Ugh. Business plans. Aren't they meant for large corporations?

I used to think so too before I took some business classes in college. Boy was I wrong. While not every business needs a 1,000 page business plan that outlines every possible scenario, detail, entity, what if, dollar figure, and aspect of their business, I believe every business or organization needs some sort of "plan."

This exercise isn't going to tell you to write a 1,000 page plan. Nor is it going to tell you to write a ten-page plan. There is no required page number to your plan, however there are some details that you should outline in your plan to start freelancing as a student.

Think of it less as a "business" plan and more of a "success" plan. A roadmap to your freelancing future, if you will. If you can plan it out on paper and it makes sense on paper, it will work out and make sense in reality. While you have all these ideas and even some plans floating around (you even possibly wrote them down in lesson 2.3), it's time to gather all of it up and formulate it into a solid plan.

While every plan will be significantly different from another, there are certain things that have to be covered, including: services offered, target market, financial expectations, initial funding, ways of marketing, etc.

The most important thing to keep in mind is this business plan is for you and you only. Unless you are looking to get a big loan from a bank or somewhere else (which is highly unlikely), this business plan is really only to help you: it will keep you motivated, focused, and allows for a greater chance of success if you actually write down what you want to do and put goals and time lines to it (more on time lines in the next lesson).

Since it is written by you and will be only for you, feel free to include anything you want in it, and write it however you want. It can be however long you want it to be. When I started January Creative, my business plan was four and a half pages, typed single spaced (or said differently, it was 1,916 words). I included headings such as my business idea and concept, target market, pricing structure, personal salary, contingency plan, marketing plan, goals, and the reasons behind renaming and relaunching my business. Very straightforward to the way I was thinking about my freelancing business.

"Hey, wait a minute, all of that sounds like things we have covered or will cover in this book!" I'm glad you caught that too! One of the main features of this book is that it will serve as your business plan! How about that?

Well, we haven't gone through all of the details yet and some will be covered later on, however, it doesn't hurt to start building the foundation of your business plan now while your ideas are flowing. This exercise will help you start thinking like a business and create the bare bones of your business plan.

DIRECTIONS: Throughout this book, we will be working on filling in the details that will essentially make up your business plan for your freelancing career as a student. However, it never hurts to go ahead and get a jump start on the planning process. On the next two pages are sections that should be included in your business plan. It's ok if you don't have all the details for each section just yet, but if you do, that is great!

Go through each section and write out the specifics according to those sections. You'll find that you won't be able to complete this exercise until you move on through the book, which is ok. Writing and planning out as much as you can now is a great way to start with the rest of the lessons in this book.

When you have reached a lesson in this book that you can add to your business plan, come back to this lesson and write the details in the lines.

(Also, feel free to type this out in the computer if you feel this is not enough space for you, or want something a bit cleaner.)

Business concept:

_____

_____

_____

_____

_____

Reasons (look back at exercise 1.3):

_____

_____

_____

_____

_____

Where you see your business in the future:

_____

_____

_____

_____

_____

Services offered and ideal client:

_____

_____

_____

_____

_____

Goals (broken down into years, if possible):

_____
_____
_____
_____
_____

Marketing plan:

_____
_____
_____
_____
_____

Financial details (i.e. personal salary, hourly rate, etc.):

_____
_____
_____
_____
_____

An added note:

We have a long way to go in this book! We started working on the business plan early to help you get a good start on creating a solid plan, but don't stop in this lesson! Every lesson you go through will give you an opportunity to add to and improve this plan. I recommend typing up your plan on the computer, and having it up and ready while you are reading through this book so that it is easier to add to during your reading. Plus, when you reach the end of the book, all you have to do is read through it, print it out and keep it with you to keep you focused and motivated toward your freelance success!

Goal Setting.

It is important not only to describe what your business will do, for whom, how much you will charge, and the like, but it is also just as important to write down in your business plan some specific goals you want to achieve. For instance: do you want your freelancing to

support you when you graduate? If so, make one of your goals "I want to be earning $X,XXX per month by the time I graduate." This will not only push you toward your goals, but keeps you focused in your freelancing, such as taking only projects you enjoy and that pay well.

2.8 Exercise Setting Up a Time Line

The big question, of course, is "when are you officially starting your business?"

When do you want to start your freelancing business? A month from now? Two months from now? If you aren't sure yet, now is a great time to finally put that big red circle on your calendar!

Why a discussion on when to start your business? Simple: having a deadline makes you more focused. Whenever you put a specific date on something, it tends to motivate you more to work hard to get it done by that date. While it is easy to simply say "I want to start my business in a couple of months," no matter how many months go by, it will always be "a couple of months."

So while you are taking on the very big project of launching your own freelance business all while tackling classes at

the same time, it's even more important to set up not only a date to where you officially hang your shingle but also develop a time line to help make sure you can meet that goal in time.

A time line for the purpose of this exercise is simply a calendar with many due dates on it. Any major project is much easier to tackle if you break it down into several smaller chunks. This lesson is going to help you break down this monster of a project into smaller chunks, then help you assign reasonable due dates to them.

A great example of a time line that you could use is staring right at you: this book! This book is divided into lessons to help you digest smaller chunks of information and exercises at a time. If you notice in the syllabus (table of contents), we actually are going to launch your freelance business by the end of lesson six, with the last four lessons being things you do after you start your business.

DIRECTIONS (Step 1): First, before coming up with any type of time line to help make your freelancing dreams a reality, you must pick a realistic "grand opening" date of your freelance business. And by realistic I mean not next week. For the amount of time involved in launching a business and the fact that you are in school for roughly eight months out of the year, your time available is a major factor in that date. With all of that in mind, when would you like to officially start your business?

My official "grand opening" for my freelance business is:

_____

Great! Is that a specific date that you can circle on a calendar, such as January 1, 2013? If so then that is great! If it isn't, then try to be more specific and assign a specific date to your grand opening.

Next, count out how many weeks you have from today's date to the date you plan to launch your freelancing business. Hopefully it is roughly six to ten weeks or more from today so you aren't slamming your schedule too much.

How many full weeks do you have until your grand opening?

_____

How many days does this equate to (take the weeks and multiply by 7)? _____

I'm going to use the way this book is laid out to help you come up with a time line, but if you are more detailed-oriented, feel free to develop your own system (be sure to break down your freelancing business launch into at least four separate deadlines).

To keep this exercise simple, let's divide out how many weeks you listed above by four. For example, say that I wrote that I have eight weeks until my grand opening, that means when I divide by four, this gives me two weeks in between each deadline. We divided by four because it is best to have four "milestones" or deadlines to help us along in the process. Feel like you would like more or less? Then feel free to divide by however many milestones you wish to have on your time line.

Let's discuss our milestones. Four is a good number of milestones to keep you motivated in any major project you may be involved in. Simply look at all the things you need to do (or the lessons in this book) and evenly divide the tasks into four equal groups. These groups are now your milestones that you can put dates to (of which we will do in the next step of this exercise).

For this lesson, it works great because we can dedicate the first three milestones to the first six lessons in this book (remember the last four lessons of this book are for after your freelancing has officially started), with the final milestone being your actual launch date. This gives you the last milestone to make sure you got all of your ducks in a row and to help cover anything you may have missed.

With that said, using the example above, I can easily say "I will go through two lessons every two weeks for each milestone, with the final two weeks and milestone being dedicated for last-minute prep."

DIRECTIONS (Step 2): Your turn! Below are lines for four milestones. Using the math involved above (and/or your own detailed-oriented plan), work out what you will do for each milestone and when each milestone is due!

Milestone 1: *Milestone 1 to be completed by:* _____

_____

_____

_____

Milestone 2: *Milestone 2 to be completed by:* _____

_____

_____

_____

Milestone 3: *Milestone 3 to be completed by:* _____

_____

_____

_____

(continued on the next page)

Milestone 4: *Milestone 4 to be completed by:* _____

_____

_____

_____

Launch my freelance business on: _____

2.9 Exam How well does your plan hold up?

Throughout this lesson, I discussed why and how you should set up a solid plan to move forward in your freelancing. How well did you think you did?

I can't stress it enough; having a strong plan going into the start of your freelancing career could make or break your successes. This is why I dedicate a very large portion of this book to planning and researching.

We talked about several things in this lesson from getting all of your ideas on paper to finding a mentor, making sure you have a financial safety net to developing a business plan. With all of this discussion and planning out the blueprint to your future freelancing success, how does your plan hold up?

DIRECTIONS: Below are statements that relate to topics about planning your freelancing career. Read each one and circle "true" or "false" based on what you have learned in this lesson.

TRUE   FALSE

 1.) It's ok to use your student loans as a financial safety net and to pay for business expenses if you need it.

 2.) Freelancers are independent, meaning that they don't seek outside help such as mentors when starting out.

T **F** 3.) Part of your business plan should include a time line, or a calendar with due dates of when you will have certain things completed for your business, including the big launch date.

T **F** 4.) While writing your own ideas down is great, you can also read through freelancing books and websites to help generate more ideas about your future freelancing business.

T **F** 5.) When starting your freelancing career as a student, it isn't important to come up with a blueprint before you officially launch your business.

T **F** 6.) If you are dependent on your job to pay your bills, you should have about six month's worth of expenses put back in case of an emergency before you start freelancing.

T **F** 7.) Once you create a business plan, or a success plan, you won't have to come back to it later on.

T **F** 8.) There are lots of things to consider when you start freelancing, even things that aren't immediately evident such as state and local taxes, insurance requirements, and developing a business plan.

T **F** 9.) When you start working on your business plan, you should cater it more to the way you think and less like a formal business plan.

T **F** 10.) There is no real need to look up industry statistics when planning your freelancing business.

SCORING: Below are the answers to the statements above. Review each one and compare them with your answers. If you answered one incorrectly, refer to the mentioned lesson to brush up on what you missed.

1.) **FALSE.** I highly recommend against using any student loan money for your freelancing, even as a financial safety net. Student loans often carry high interest rates, and any money you use now you will have to pay back later plus some. Find other ways to build your financial safety net, such putting money back from your current job or talk to your parents or spouse about your decision to freelance to see if they are able to help be your financial safety net. *LESSON 2.6*

2.) **FALSE.** While some freelancers never seek help from mentors in the early part of their careers, those that do often benefit in saving time by quickly learning what they need to do and what to expect than if they were to research out this information on their own. Mentors range from professors to other freelancers, even business professionals. *LESSON 2.5*

3.) **TRUE.** Developing and keeping to a time line makes you focused on meeting your goal of launching on a specific date. Often when we don't set deadlines for ourselves, we put off certain things and never dedicate time to get things done. Don't let this happen to you by not making a time line to follow during your freelance planning. *LESSON 2.7*

4.) **TRUE.** We discussed writing down all of your ideas about freelancing as they come to you so you can not only keep from forgetting them but so you can reference these ideas later on. In addition, you can refer to freelancing books and websites to drum up new ideas or things to consider as you start your journey as a freelancer. *LESSON 2.3*

5.) **FALSE.** The main idea in this lesson was all about creating a plan and mapping out everything you need to do before you can start freelancing. When you take time to develop a plan, you are more likely to follow through and become more successful than starting without any plan. *LESSON 2.1*

6.) **TRUE.** You have no one else but yourself to depend on to pay these bills. You should start working now to put back money until you reach the equivalent of six months worth of your expenses. However, for students who have their daily expenses covered by some other method (parents, spouse, etc.), they can get away with having less as a financial safety net. *LESSON 2.6*

7.) **FALSE.** What's the point of making one if you will never use it? Your business plan, throughout the entire time you are planning your freelance business, will change and morph into a more complete plan, one that you will be able to use throughout the launch and early part of your freelancing career. *LESSON 2.7*

8.) **TRUE.** Most student freelancers focus on the most noticeable things about a business, such as what to charge and how to get clients. However, there are also other things that are just as important that needs attention as well, some of which become apparent after a student has started doing research about freelancing. This book is designed to help you learn about those hidden aspects of student freelancing. *LESSON 2.2*

9.) **TRUE.** Chances are you're the only one that will see your business plan, so why make it more complicated than it should be? Even though you can format and organize it however you wish, don't forget to include the big topics such as your target market, financial expectations, marketing tools, and services you will offer. *LESSON 2.7*

10.) **FALSE.** Researching your industry and looking up freelancing statistics can give you a clearer picture of what to expect when you start freelancing. It can also help guide you in the decisions you are about to make, such as what field(s) of freelancing you can pursue and if they are profitable, how those in your age group are faring as freelancers, and even how much you should charge for your services. *LESSON 2.4*

GRADE: Want to grade yourself on how you did? Below is how you can grade your performance in this exam.

How many you got right: _____ Divided by 10 = _____ x 100 = _____ %

Example: Answered 9 right. 9 / 10 = .9 x 100 = 90%

What's next in line?

In the next lesson, we are going to be talking about many of the not-so-fun things involving your freelancing, including a business name, seeking help of professional advisors, business formation, taxes, contracts, and other legal issues. While it isn't fun to deal with these things, not getting a handle on them now could cause problems for you later on. See you in the next lesson!

Lesson 3

Legal Matters

Let's face it; talking about legal stuff is not fun. Anything from contracts to taxes would make any freelancer nervous, let alone a starting student freelancer with limited experience with these topics. While it isn't fun to talk about, it is a vital part of your freelance success.

In this lesson, we will tackle some of the legal issues you will run into head-on. We start with picking a business name then move into the information about taxes you should be aware of. We will then end the lesson discussing contracts and start working on your freelancing contract.

3.1 Lecture Staying on the Straight and Narrow

No one likes dealing with all the legal stuff, but if you don't, you could find yourself in a lot of hot water.

I want to first start off with a disclaimer: I am not a lawyer, accountant, or by any means a business consultant. The information I give in this section is to be a starting place only to give you an idea of what you need to look for under these certain topics.

Having some sort of idea of what to expect when it comes to the legal side of freelancing is crucial so that you can make sure you are legal where you live and hopefully avoid getting into some trouble later on.

Also, most of what I will say throughout this lesson is directed toward those living in the United States. If you live in a different country, you will need to see what the equivalent is for that country and any additional legal requirements you are responsible for.

With that said, in this lesson, I will provide a quick overview of some of the legal stuff you will need to get hammered down and be aware of when you start freelancing. Some of the topics include taxes, contracts, business formation, and other legal issues.

These things are vitally important to your business. For instance, without contracts you open yourself up to risks without any protection. What if a client decides not to pay you? Your contract could save you in that case, as being something you can reference to make sure you get paid.

While talking about all the legal stuff isn't fun, I should stress again that every business has to deal with these legal aspects of their business. Thus, it just makes good business sense to tackle these issues head-on and make sure they

> *No one likes to deal with the legal side of freelancing, but protecting yourself now could pay off later.*

are all taken care of to protect you and your growing freelance business while you are in school and after you graduate and continue your freelancing.

Seeking and Securing Professional Advisors.

Hindsight is always 20/20, but after being a freelancer for five years and recently relaunching my business, I can appreciate the importance of getting professional help. Since we are going to be talking about many legal issues that you nor I know much about, it is always in your best interest if you plan to start freelancing while you are in school, that you should seek professional help. Such help includes at the bare minimum a lawyer and an accountant. Others may include an insurance agent, business coach, and others. Take time now to find a good lawyer and a good accountant that you feel comfortable with and that works with the types of businesses you are wanting to start with your freelancing. Plus, don't be afraid to ask for a student discount either; just because you are a student doesn't mean that such professional help should be unavailable to you due to budget constraints!

3.2 Lecture Personal Name or Business Name?

There comes a time in every freelancer's life where they have to decide, "should I operate under my own name or come up with a business name instead?"

With positives and negatives to each, the student freelancer must first decide how long they intend on being a freelancer. When most freelancers start freelancing, they fall into freelancing with no real plan. Thus, they tend to operate under their own name such as "Amber Turner Creative," like I did. Once they decide they want to continue their freelancing for the long term, they often come up with a business name to operate under.

If you believe your freelancing is a short-term thing, working under your own name works best. However, if you have big hopes and dreams and see this new career path as a long-term endeavor, coming up with a business name is more appropriate.

Like I said earlier, there are benefits and disadvantages with each option. While freelancing under your own name helps make your freelancing feel more personal, a business name would make you seem more professional. The following is a list of pros and cons for each option to help you decide if a personal name or business name is best for your new freelancing career.

Personal Name

Pros:

- You will appear more personal to clients, as it is your name on the door.
- Certain fields, such as photography and accounting, actually benefit more from using a personal name over a business name.
- You are your reputation: when you work with clients, how you perform is directly tied to your name, not your business name.
- It is often easier for clients to recall your name and find you later on.
- It is ideal if you plan to stay a solo business or don't plan on freelancing for a long time.
- This may also be a good option if you have decided to freelance only while in school.

Cons:

- Clients may see you as not being as professional as someone operating under a business name.
- It could cause you many headaches and confusion if you have a very common name such as "John Smith."
- You also may run into issues if you have a hard-to-pronounce name.

- You may have a hard time hiring employees if you start to grow past the point of your own abilities.
- You are more likely to run into issues if you should ever change your name, such as in the event of marriage and/or divorce (for the ladies).

Business Name

Pros:

- You will appear more long-term and stable to clients when you set up shop under a business name.
- It helps you keep your personal and business life separate.
- It is easier to sell your freelancing business should you decide not to continue your self-employment.
- It is best if you have a very common name and/or hard-to-pronounce name and choosing a personal name may not be feasible.
- A business name allows you the option to hire employees if you start to grow and need help.
- It is a good route should you feel your name could change in the future, such as getting married and/or divorced (mainly for women).
- Overall allows more flexibility to operate your freelancing as a business.

Cons:

- There is a greater chance that someone could already be using the business name you come up with.
- Depending on where you live, there may be some extra paperwork involved when declaring your business name.
- If clients know you by name, you may be a little more difficult to find you when operating under a business name (unless they found your business first).

- It is often harder to tell the size of your business, which could hurt you if your clients are looking for a small firm and you appear to be really big.
- The chance of legal ramifications increase, even if you were unaware, when operating under a business name that is already being used.

3.3 Exercise Brainstorming Business Names

Now that we know the pros and cons to each type of business name, here comes the fun part!

Coming up with and deciding on a name in which you will operate can be exciting, difficult, creative, a pain, or all of the above. In the last section we talked about coming up with a name and the different types of names you could come up with (either a personal name or business name).

I'm sure you're excited to start the process and already have some ideas! This lesson will help you brainstorm name ideas and determine which ones have potential and which

ones should be discarded. At the end of the exercise you should have a clear picture on what name will work best for you (or pretty close to making that decision).

DIRECTIONS (PART 1): Looking back at the reasons and motives behind why you want to start freelancing (that you came up with in lesson 1), decide on how long you intend on freelancing. Is it something just to get you through school, or is it a career path you intend to keep after graduation? Do you want to continue running your business for the majority of your life or do you see yourself starting your business to sell at a later time?

I intend on freelancing for (state a time period):

_____

_____
_____
_____
_____
_____
_____

Tips on Choosing a Business Name

Once you have a nice list of names to choose from, it is time to start narrowing down the list so that you can pick the best one for you and your business. Below are a few tips that will help you with that process.

Search for available domain names (example: amberturner. com). This may help you narrow down the amount of choices to pick from.

Make sure you can live with the decision; it may be best to sit on that name for days, weeks, or even months.

DIRECTIONS (PART 2): After deciding if a personal or business name is appropriate, start brainstorming name ideas. This could take a while, as it took me over a year to decide on a business name. Below are lines to help you keep your thoughts organized.

Once you start becoming serious about a name option, hurry up and grab the available domain name(s), Twitter handles, Skype names, etc so that no one else claims them before you do.

DIRECTIONS (PART 3): Work toward getting a list of five to ten solid options for business names. There are lines to the right to write them down. Then, as you go through this book and work on planning your freelancing career, revisit this list and start narrowing them down even more. You will eventually find a name that suits you well!

_____

_____

_____

_____

_____

_____

_____

_____

_____

_____

_____

_____

Business Formation.

Not familiar with business formations, such as sole proprietorship, LLC, or C- and S-corp? Most freelancers will organize under a sole proprietorship which will not require any formal business filing (in most cases). However, if you become anything more than a sole proprietor (such as a corporation or a limited liability corporation), you will need both a lawyer and accountant to help you file the necessary paperwork. Talk with a legal and accounting professional to find out which organization best aligns with your freelancing goals, type of freelancing, and how long you anticipate on being a freelancer. They will guide you in the right direction. You can learn more about the differences between a sole proprietorship, partnership, LLC, and different forms of corporations by doing a quick Google search.

3.4 Lecture The Dreaded 'T' Word

Taxes. Yep, that dreaded word. What do you need to know about taxes before you start freelancing as a student?

Let's start with a very big topic and something that often comes up first for student freelancers. When you start freelancing, you become self-employed in the eyes of the IRS. This means you not only pay your portion of taxes, but you must pay the employer side of taxes as well.

When you are working for someone else, they have to pay the same amount of taxes that they automatically take out of your paycheck (FICA, Social Security, and Medicare). However, when you are self-employed, you are both the employee and employer.

So when you start working for clients, you should be aware that you will no longer be getting a refund from the IRS and that you will owe quite a bit at the end of the year. To help with this, you should take roughly 20-25% of every payment from a client and put back into your savings and don't touch it until you need to write a check to the IRS.

There are also estimated taxes you need to be aware of. After your first year, you should start paying estimated taxes. This is basically filing a very short tax return every quarter. The IRS wants you to pay estimated quarterly taxes to help reduce the amount you owe at the end of the year. If you don't do this, then you could get penalized on your federal tax return.

You may also have to pay state, county, and city taxes for being a business owner. A phone call to your local department of revenue, secretary of state, or other office that handles filings for businesses can help you find out about the requirements. Some of those requirements include sales tax, business taxes, and other necessary taxes that pertain to where you live.

Seek help from an accountant with anything to do with your taxes. DO NOT ATTEMPT to do your own taxes as it will greatly increase your chances of being audited. Also, a discussion with your accountant will help you plan for your

federal tax bill at the end of the year (and if you should be saving more than 25% for taxes), and help you even reduce your tax liability with things such as business expenses.

Other Legal Issues.

Just because you have everything squared away with your taxes and you are about to work on your contract, that doesn't mean you are good to go in the legal sense. Additionally, you will need to find out if you need to get a business license and if you have to charge sales tax. An accountant is invaluable at this stage, since every locality is different. They will also direct you in what is appropriate for you in other aspects of your business as well. Last but not least, you will have legal issues such as contracts that you need to be aware of. Work with a lawyer to develop a contract that you can use for your freelancing. We will discuss more about contracts next.

3.5 Lecture How and Why to Use Contracts

It comes as a surprise to some, while others are aware of them; contracts are those necessary things that no freelancer likes deal with, but all appreciate that they are there.

I didn't start using contracts for my freelancing until at least a year into it. Why? I didn't know I needed them and didn't see the importance behind them. Plus, to me it always made me very uncomfortable. I know I'm not the only one, as most freelancers starting out don't like them either and often go without one.

That is until something goes wrong. Contracts developed by freelancers for their clients are used to protect them from anything that could go wrong during a project. It also helps to outline responsibilities and project details such as pricing and deliverables. The most important reason why freelancers have contracts with their clients is because it is the professional thing to do.

For those that have not been in business for long or are unfamiliar, contracts are a way of doing business these days, and for good reason. Since they set a professional atmosphere in which both parties (or all parties) in the contract can work, they are used quite a bit in pretty much any form of business. For freelancers, contracts help show their professionalism when dealing with a client, while outlining project details and protect themselves during and after a client project.

Contracts shouldn't be all bad though. They can often be used for other benefits. For instance, contracts have been used as a way to help land projects, instead of something that takes place after a verbal agreement. Other freelancers use it as an educational tool as well, including more information about the project they are going to work on for the client.

Whatever your feelings are about contracts, you should realize and come to terms with the fact that they are a required necessity in most fields of freelancing. Although I am not a lawyer, I would have to say that any project dealing with large sums of money, copyrights and intellectual property, or has high legal ramifications if something goes wrong are projects that a contract is definitely needed for. Make developing and using contracts a high priority in your freelancing business so that you can always stay safe.

3.6 Exercise Developing a Working Contract

Contracts are tricky, but developing one is even trickier. Let's go over some ways in which you can start developing a contract for your services.

Unfortunately, there is no sure-fire way to develop a contract. There is no proven method to develop one. And even after you get a contract into place and you start having clients sign it, you will inevitably start finding things that you want to add, change, or remove from future editions of your contract. There isn't one freelancer that can tell you that they haven't changed their contract at least once in their career.

Every contract should have some bare-bones information, such as clients names, project details, payment information, copyright information, how any type of conflict will be resolved, and a place for signatures. But what types of other information should be included in your contract?

Not only do you have to make sure you have everything covered, you also need to structure your contract so that it is a contract. You don't have to have all of the lawyer-speak in it to have a contract, but it does need to be written in a way so that it is taken seriously.

In this exercise, we are going to start working on developing a working contract. What I mean by a "working contract" is one that you are building and polishing before you start using it with potential clients. Consider it as your rough draft. This should be one that you start putting together in order to have a lawyer review it. Your contract is only considered "complete" once it has either been reviewed by a lawyer or you are confident that you have everything covered in the contract relating to the services you offer.

The best way to develop your own contract and understand the importance of developing one is to just start researching, finding, and reading contract templates, examples and clauses that others have put out there for you to use as examples to help educate yourself. Every freelancer has had to take time to research contracts relating to the work they do, and it is the single, best way to get a crash course in reading, creating, and presenting contracts to clients.

DIRECTIONS: It is time to start putting together a working contract, but before you can do that, you need to start researching examples of contracts so that you know what should be in your contract, how it should be structured, and why certain parts should be in your freelancing contract.

First, start off by doing some Googling for terms such as "graphic design contract," "freelance web design agreement," or "freelance photographer contract template." Depending on your field of freelancing, you can use any combination of the words above along with words involving your field of freelancing (writer, developer, photographer, etc.). There are plenty of resources online where you can find templates and examples of contracts. Look for the best examples and bookmark them for the second part of this exercise.

Now it is time to start putting all the pieces together. On a separate sheet of paper, in a blank document on your computer, or some other fashion, start looking for an writing down similarities in all the contracts you found. You should see that all of the contracts will have client's name, your name, address and contact information, pricing and project information, copyright information, and a place for signatures. Make note of all the sections that are the same in every contract example/template you found.

Next, start looking at the templates and examples you found and find things that you feel are important to include in your own agreement. For example, since I offer web hosting services to my clients, I felt it was important to explain "the rules" where it comes to hosting, such as "don't host copyrighted work on your server" and "don't put anything illicit or illegal on the server." This is to protect me in case my clients do decide to partake in such activities.

Other information you may find that you want to include is license information. As a photographer, this may be of importance to you. Will your clients be able to have full, unlimited use of the images you create, or can they only use it for one specific purpose?

Going through the template and example contracts will take some time, but it is an important step to protect not only your work, but you as well where it comes to your relationship with your clients, your income, and your freelancing business.

Once you have your contract complete and you feel you have exhausted all the things you should have in your contract, proofread it very well, make sure the organization of the contract makes sense (i.e. don't put the conflict resolution section before the project scope section, signatures go at the end), and either have your lawyer review it or at the very least your mentor or freelancer friend read over it. Keep in mind, your contract is a legal, binding document and it is HIGHLY recommended that you hire a lawyer to review your contract to make sure it legally protects you the way you intend for it to, along with getting any additional advice on additional clauses that should be added to your contract.

3.7 Exam Do you have all of your legal ducks in a row?

Getting all of the legal stuff taken care of for your business is no easy task, but do you have everything done and ready to set up shop?

We covered a lot of ground in this chapter. Everything from picking a name to operate under, taxes and what you can expect, even down to discussing a large part of your future freelance business—contracts. I also highlighted many times the need to hire a professional or two to help you with legal and accounting needs as well.

Even though we talked about all of these things, are you really ready to move forward with getting your freelance business going? Below are several questions to help you evaluate your current legal stance where it comes to moving on in this book.

DIRECTIONS: Each of the following statements relate to things discussed in this lesson. Answer each one by circling "true" or "false" to measure your knowledge of the legal matters in this lesson.

TRUE   FALSE

  1.) In addition to filing your federal taxes, you may have to start paying quarterly estimated taxes during the year to avoid penalties.

(T) (F) 2.) One benefit of choosing a personal name over a business name for your freelance business is that clients will see you as a professional.

(T) (F) 3.) Once you make your contract, you should never have to change it as your freelancing changes and grows.

(T) (F) 4.) There are pros and cons to selecting either a personal name or a business name for your freelancing.

(T) (F) 5.) Every student freelancer should use the exact same contract to make it easier for clients to work with them on projects.

(T) (F) 6.) Freelancers don't have many legal hoops to jump through, so seeking advice from and hiring lawyers and accountants isn't necessary.

(T) (F) 7.) One of the decisions in choosing a business name (be it a personal name or an actual business name) is to check to see if it has an available domain name that matches or is similar to the business name.

(T) (F) 8.) Being a freelancer and self-employed, you don't have to pay the same taxes as those who are employed and receive a paycheck do.

(T) (F) 9.) When picking a name to operate under, it often helps to determine how long you plan to be a freelancer.

(T) (F) 10.) When developing your contract, there is no need to see how others have put theirs together.

SCORING: How well did you think you did? Check your answers against the explanations on the next several pages to see how well you know the legal side of freelancing.

1.) **TRUE.** Depending on your situation, chances are you will have to pay taxes throughout the year based on how much you made the year before. A discussion with your accountant is the best way to set up your estimated payments. Failure to set up estimated tax payments when you are required to could result in penalties when you file your taxes. *LESSON 3.4*

2.) **FALSE.** This may work in some professions, but for those who are self-employed freelancers, this is not necessarily the case. Clients often see businesses as more professional over individuals and are more likely to hire a business than an individual in most fields of freelancing. *LESSON 3.2*

3.) **FALSE.** We talked about developing a working contract because you will often find things you need to add or change in your contract. Since most student freelancers often don't have experience in contracts, there can be holes in your contract that only become visible with time and use. *LESSON 3.6*

4.) **TRUE.** There is really no clear answer to which one is better: a personal name or a business name. Each have their own benefits and drawbacks that need to be considered. How these benefits and drawbacks impact a student's current situation and future goals is often what determines which is the best for them. *LESSON 3.2*

5.) **FALSE.** Contracts are meant to protect the freelancer and are often crafted in a way that is specific to how the freelancer works. You should make your contract work for the way you want to run your freelancing business, not how others have their contracts. Also, remember that they should follow the laws in your area and common practices. *LESSON 3.5*

6.) **FALSE.** No matter what business you start, you should always consult professional advisors such as lawyers and accountants. They can often bring to light issues you may not have been aware of and they work to keep you protected and in the legal right when it comes to things such as contracts and taxes. *LESSON 3.1*

7.) **TRUE.** No matter if you are picking a personal name or business name, it is imperative that you find a domain name that you can host your website. This domain name needs to match or is some how connected to your actual name, for example *Students That Freelance* has a domain name of studentsthatfreelance.com. *LESSON 3.3*

8.) **FALSE.** Not only do you still have to pay your share of federal taxes such as FICA and Medicare, you also get to pay the employer's share as well, meaning you pay close to double what is taken out of an employee's paycheck before they receive them. Because of this, it is important to plan accordingly and store around 25% of your income in the savings for when your tax bill comes due. *LESSON 3.4*

9.) **TRUE.** Some students want to freelance only while they are in college, while others intend to make it their career after graduation. These intents can really make an impact on if you should operate under your name or come up with a business name. *LESSON 3.3*

10.) **FALSE.** Although contracts should be designed to help protect you and ensure clients understand what is going on, student freelancers who don't have much experience in contracts (reading or creating them) should become familiar with what is in others' contracts to help them create their own. If and when you do this, however, just be sure to keep your contract focused on how you run your business. *LESSON 3.6*

GRADE: If you are keeping count, you can calculate your grade using the formula below.

How many you got right: _____ Divided by 10 = _____ x 100 = _____ %

Example: Answered 10 right. 10 / 10 = 1 x 100 = 100%

What can you expect next?

There are tons of stuff still to cover in this book. In the next lesson, it is all about setting up your business such as determining your services, discovering your ideal client and creating a profile for your target market, developing and fine-tuning your portfolio, creating your work schedule, setting up your office, and how to keep and maintain good records. Sounds like a lot, so we better get started! See you in the next lesson!

Lesson 4

Setting Up Shop

This is where the real fun begins, in my opinion. In this lesson we will cover the big things that you have been waiting for, such as determining your services, figuring out what type of client is your ideal client, getting your portfolio together, setting up your schedule, and more.

Setting up shop is one of the most exciting parts in starting your freelancing career. Because of this, we will cover quite a few things in this lesson, but I am confident that you will have some fun with the things discussed here. Without further adieu, time to start having real fun!

4.1 Exercise Determining Your Services

What exactly are you going to do for clients that come to you wanting work?

Every freelancer has a general list of services they want to offer to clients. The reasons to have a list of services that you offer is large, but mainly includes the following: knowing what you can do off-hand should a client ask you, allows you to focus on getting only that type of work, and helps you to start building a portfolio toward the type of work you want to do the most.

Taking some time to discover and determine which services in your field of freelancing you will be offering will help you market yourself better and take on projects that best fit your skills.

DIRECTIONS: Start writing down the types of work you like to do for the type of freelancing you are wanting to pursue. For instance, a graphic designer may want to stick to only publication design such as brochures, catalogues, and programs, but may not want to do logo design. This graphic designer would then list their services as "publication design, including brochure design, catalogue design, and program design." List the services you intend to offer in the spaces below, along with the types of work associated with each service.

_____

_____

_____

_____

_____

Since you probably wrote down many different types of services above, in the lines on the next page, finalize the services you wish to offer. Be sure to keep your list fairly brief: aim for around 5 types of services or less. Also, list the ones you do not want to offer at the bottom, just so you know when clients start asking you what you offer and what you don't offer.

_____
_____
_____
_____
_____
_____
_____
_____
_____
_____
_____
_____
_____
_____

Additional Streams of Income.

Most freelancers will tell you they have several streams of income other than just their primary freelancing business. For instance, some web designers sell designs on sites like ThemeForest.net, web developers sell ongoing services like hosting, or like yours truly, create a product relating to their freelancing and sell it. Maybe you are a great photographer who has an itch to teach others and share your skill? You could either write for photography blogs or set up special sessions and teach beginning photographers how to capture amazing shots. With all of this said, it helps to have multiple streams of income to help support you when one of the streams may be running a little dry. While you think about the services you offer, also think about what could be considered an additional stream of income and what should be in your main set of services.

4.2 Exercise Discovering and Creating Your Ideal Client Profile and Target Market

Who exactly are you wanting to conduct business with? Who would benefit from your services the most?

Tons of questions to be asked, with tons of answers to be determined. Most freelancers have to go through the process of discovering their target market. What we are going to do is develop an ideal client profile. Basically, you need to figure out who needs your services, who you want to work with, and where would they be most of the time.

The reason this is an important step has something to do with a shotgun. Didn't expect that, huh? Well, when a shotgun is fired, you have all of these pieces of metal that come flying out, they are all going to hit something at different times and different places, and could often lead to missing your target all together.

Most freelancers and those unfamiliar with marketing concepts start off doing something very similar to a shotgun. When you don't have a clear target of who you are wanting to market to you end up sending marketing materials everywhere and never really landing anything. This not only leads to very little return on your marketing efforts, but is highly inefficient and could eventually end up being quite expensive.

Developing your ideal client profile will allow you to target your marketing efforts toward specific people, which in turn greatly increases the chance of making a "hit." Said another way, if you are a photographer who focuses on wedding photography, sending your marketing message to every female in your city is a wasted effort because more than likely half of those women are already married, a quarter will be too young to be getting married, and most of who are left are either not even in a relationship, not engaged, or already have a wedding photographer for their upcoming wedding. However, if the wedding photographer starts targeting their messages to brides, then they are more likely to land business out of those starting to plan their weddings because they would be in the right mindset to acquire photography for their big day.

Keeping with the idea of a wedding photographer, we are going to start working on your ideal client profile and target market. Your ideal client profile will consist of all the aspects of the perfect client in your eyes, while the target market will be those who fit most, if not all, of the aspects of your ideal client profile. Let's get started!

DIRECTIONS: First off, you must determine who you would consider your ideal client. What characteristics do they have that would make them your perfect client?

Continuing with the wedding photographer example, their ideal client would be those who are currently engaged and who are in the beginning stages of planning their wedding.

Taking the services you listed in the last section, think about who would be best suited for the services you offer. Who would be most likely (in a perfect world) to hire you for your services? What characteristics would they have (i.e. budget, where they are located, how often they need those services, why they need those services, how you can help them, etc.). List those characteristics on the next page.

_____

_____

_____

Now that you have a rough idea of your ideal client, where can these people be found most often either through physical or digital means?

Continuing with our example, those that are connected with the wedding industry would be a great place to start,

such as bridal shops, wedding planners, bridal shows, etc. Also, newly-engaged couples may be looking in wedding magazines and/or online for wedding ideas.

List the locations where your ideal client would likely be found below. This is considered your target market.

_____

_____

_____

4.3 Quiz How Well Do You Really Know Your Potential Clients?

You could mind read, guess, major in psychology, ask tons of people, or a combination of the aforementioned, but understanding your potential clients is hard work and takes lots of researching and discovering.

We all sit back and think we know what potential clients want and what they are thinking, but the truth is, we don't. If we all knew what clients were thinking and what they wanted, there would be no need for marketing.

In the last section, we developed what we believe is our ideal client profile, but we could still be wrong. For marketers, one of the most enjoyable, albeit frustrating parts of their job is figuring out their target market. So with all of the work we did in the last section, how well do you know your potential clients, or the clients that you want to target your marketing to?

DIRECTIONS: Here is a list of questions to ask yourself about your ideal client. Going through each one, ask yourself each question and truthfully answer it. If you get stuck or are struggling on a question, now is a good time to do some research and answer that question with confidence. I have given you some lines so that you can write down the answer to each question, just to make sure you have all of your thoughts in one place.

1.) Where do those in the industry in which your ideal client participates often look for the services you offer? Do they turn to the web, or look through directories? Is it more word-of-mouth or do they best respond to direct mail?

_____

_____

_____

2.) What are their overall attitudes toward the services you offer? Are they always hiring for services you provide or do they only need your service every now and then? Do they generally respect those in your profession or feel as though you don't do something of significant value (meaning, are they looking for a professional or someone just to do the grunt work)?

_____

_____

_____

3.) Is your target client already knowledgeable about the services you offer, or do they need some education and assistance along the way? How much (or how little) education would be needed in order to land projects with your ideal target market?

_____

_____

_____

4.) Are the ideal clients able to afford the services you are providing? Would a project with you require them to seek additional approval before spending money, or would they be able to make the decision without going through mounds of red tape? Is there only one sole person responsible for all the budget decisions, or is this often left to a group?

_____

_____

_____

5.) How large is the industry(ies) that your ideal clients participate in? Is it a growing industry or a dying industry? Is the industry severely fragmented into several different kinds or types or is it pretty close around the same type of work? How is competition in those industries among other similar companies to your ideal client's company; is it fierce or nonexistent?

_____

_____

_____

Tough questions, huh? Not every freelancer can accurately and sufficiently answer each question to the fullest, not even seasoned ones, so it's ok if you are unsure. The main object of this quiz is to get you thinking about all the things you can research about your potential clients and ideal target market so you are able to better connect with them and market your services with them.

The more you know about them, the more comfortable they will feel when hiring you, the more willing they will be to chat with you about their needs, and the more professional you will appear to your ideal target market.

4.4 Lecture The All-Important Portfolio

For most fields of freelancing, your portfolio will make or break any chances you have at freelancing success.

Your portfolio is THE most important thing you need to start freelancing. If you can't show your potential clients what you have done in the past, with confidence, then why should they hire you? Since your portfolio of work is the most important thing, I am dedicating two sections in this book to everything you need to know about developing your portfolio.

Having had to work on my portfolio about five times a year every year for the past five years (so a little math would make that 25 times since I started freelancing), I have learned that there are certain elements and issues relating to portfolios that starting student freelancers should be aware of.

First off, they need to be well representative of the work you wish to be hired to do. If you're a graphic designer who wants to do mainly logo design, having most of your portfolio as websites is a real disconnect. Your portfolio should focus around what you do best and the services you want to offer (these should be one in the same, or very close to one another). Also, just because you are an excellent artist and you are a photographer offering

wedding photography services doesn't mean your clients will want to see your drawings.

Keeping your portfolio up-to-date is vital as well. Since you are constantly producing new work and learning new skills,

Your portfolio is the most important thing you need to start freelancing because you have to be able to show your potential clients what you can do.

what you are working on now, and have been working on is almost guaranteed to be better than what you had in your portfolio. You want your clients to see the best work you have produced in order to give them the most accurate picture of what they can expect when they hire you. It also helps justify the amount you are charging for the services they are requesting (no worries, we will get more into what to charge later in this lesson).

Depending on the field of freelancing you are going to be involved in, you may need only a printed portfolio (physical), only a web portfolio (digital), or a combination of both. Web designers will likely be able to get away with only a digital portfolio, where as writers may need both a physical one along with some web presence that will have their works displayed as well.

However, the way your clients are going to see your work is how you need to display it. If they are likely to find you online, then a digital portfolio is best, but if they are going to want you to come by and bring it in for them to see, then you need a physical portfolio for those situations.

Don't overrepresent yourself in your portfolio either. Don't put in pieces that you can't confidently do in the future. Clients will be able to tell if you are trying to overrepresent yourself and it will make you look bad, causing you not to get hired. On the other end, don't underrepresent what you can do either. Clients want to know how you can help them, so if you show you have great marketing skills that go with your design skills, show them this in your portfolio as well.

Label everything you have in your portfolio clearly and concisely. You need to write down details such as the date, who it was for (either school project, personal project, or a paying client), any media and/or software involved, and the size of the piece (if it is a printed piece). It also wouldn't hurt to write a very brief description (about two sentences or 25 words) about the piece so that a client can read and understand your involvement in the project. Remember, your client is looking for these details.

So with portfolios being the most important thing you will need to start freelancing, it's essential that a decent amount of time needs to be spent making sure it is well prepared, well presented, and is correctly formatted for the method of delivery you intend (physical or digital).

Also, make sure you have your portfolio together and complete ahead of time. You don't want to spend all night getting your portfolio together to show a client because you are more likely to make mistakes and put it together with less care than something you spend a week working on and preparing.

While putting together your portfolio can be stressful (and the tips I have shared in this lesson don't help ease the stress I'm sure), remember to be creative in how you put your portfolio together. You are a creative individual so if you go against the norm some with presenting your portfolio, it could help you stand out among the crowd of other freelancers and students that your client is looking to hire. Don't go too crazy though as that could keep you from landing any paying clients and cause some hurt feelings from rejection. Have fun, but stay professional and concise!

4.5 Exercise Getting Your Portfolio in Order

After reading the long lecture on do's and don'ts when it comes to your portfolio, now it's time to put them into action to get your portfolio ready to go.

Taking all the tips you read in the last lecture, now is the time to start thinking about the work you have and which are suitable for your portfolio. Not every piece of work you have will go in your portfolio. It is best to choose your best work, the work that is most closely aligned with the services you offer, and the ones you feel the most confident about.

DIRECTIONS: Pull out, dust off and put together your portfolio of work. Keep in mind all of the do's and don'ts listed on the last couple of pages. Depending on how long you have been producing work, you may have a lot or a little to choose from. In either case, pull your pieces out and decide which will make it to your portfolio and which will not. I have provided some lines on the next page to help you organize what pieces will go in your portfolio.

Once you have your pieces pulled together, format them so they will fit either your physical or digital portfolio. If your work is physical and you need to get it ready for digital, photograph (in high-resolution or RAW format) the work and make sure it is as accurate as possible to the original piece. If your work is digital and you need to make it physical, create a folder and start adding your work to that folder so you can work on printing them later (remember, high-resolution images!).

Start writing out the details for each piece. You can write them in the blanks on the next page as well. Be sure to include the following details about each piece:

- Title of the work.
- Client's name.
- Date of completion.
- Medium/media (i.e. digital print, website, ink on paper, digital media).
- Size(s) of the piece(s) if it's a physical work.
- Brief write up about the work.
- Other specific information relating to the work, such as a URL for a website, a partnership with someone else (if you didn't do all the work yourself), any particular programs or software used (i.e. Adobe Illustrator, HTML/CSS, WordPress...), etc.

_____

_____

_____

_____

_____

_____

_____

_____

_____

_____

_____

_____

_____

_____

_____

_____

_____

Keeping Your Portfolio Up-To-Date.

It took a lot of work to get your portfolio together and ready to show potential clients. Don't let that hard work go to waste! Even though you have finished getting your portfolio together for now, it doesn't mean you have stopped creating new works and it definitely does not mean you have stopped improving your skill set. At a minimum, you should update your portfolio every other month. Add new pieces you are proud of and potential clients would be interested in seeing to possibly hire you to do for them. Go through the work you do have in your portfolio and look to see if any of your pieces are not relevant anymore or starting to look "dated." Also, if you find yourself leaning toward one type of work, start focusing your portfolio toward that line of work. The most important thing is to always keep your portfolio fresh and updated—even it means creating side projects or doing projects for close friends and family.

4.6 Exercise Creating Your Work (and Life) Schedule

The time you have available for freelancing outside of all of your other obligations is going to be limited with the busy schedules that most students have.

Due to the fact that students are very busy, it becomes even more vital for a student freelancer to have a set schedule for when they are going to do certain activities and how long they will do them for.

If your schedule varies widely from day to day, making a weekly schedule would be more beneficial. However, if your schedule is roughly the same Monday through Friday, creating a daily schedule should work better. If you are extremely detail-oriented, you may find a combination of the two to be more helpful.

Either way, think about how your current schedule is laid out and when you could fit freelancing into that schedule. Also, do you tend to do things when you feel like it or do you actually sit down and do work when you should be and when you had planned to do it? These are things that can help you create a schedule in which you can follow to make sure that you can meet all of your obligations and responsibilities as college students where it comes to grades and your personal life.

There are some key points to remember when trying to formulate a schedule you plan to keep. First, make sure you include the time it takes to get ready, travel time, time for study, chores, sleeping, and eating. These are often forgotten activities and can easily be missed when creating a workable schedule of activities for a freelancer.

Look for large chunks of time you can dedicate solely to one activity or another if you don't have a set time to do a specific thing. Blocks of three hours where you can consistently work is a great period of time to get something done for either school or your freelancing business. Also, at the end of three hours you are more than likely wanting to change it up and do something different.

DIRECTIONS: Decide on what type of schedule would be best for your situation. Is every single day pretty much the same from day to day or do you have a class schedule that is drastically different from day to day?

On a separate piece of paper, do one of the following:

- If your schedule is the same day after day, then write out each hour of the day, starting at the time you wake up (or should wake up) and ending at the time you go to bed (or should go to bed). Write in all your classes and obligations that have set times every single day. Now map out the time it takes you to get ready to leave and commute to those obligations.
- If your schedule is different from day to day, make columns on your paper for each day of the week. In each column, follow the same method as above.

Once you have the obligations that you cannot move mapped out, start looking for large chunks of free time (three hours or more of free time). Found some? Awesome! Mark those with boxes.

From here, it is really up to you how you want to use these large blocks of time (and the other blocks of free time that you didn't mark above). Should you use them to study? Can you use some of them for only freelance work?

With each person's situation being different, use your best judgement to map out your schedule including when you will be freelancing. Afterwards, start treating these times as your work schedule just like you would if you were employed elsewhere. These are times you absolutely must use for freelancing unless something major happens.

4.7 Exercise Getting Your Office Organized

You will see a trend throughout this book: organization. An organized freelancer is a happy freelancer, and it starts with your office.

Before you can start your freelancing career as a student, you have to make sure everything is organized and ready to go. Do you have all the required tools to help you complete projects? Is your office space a mess or is it well organized? Does your work environment promote or hinder productivity? All of these and more are things we will discuss in this exercise.

There are three key areas to think about when it comes to your office and making sure it is organized: office space, office arrangement, and office supplies. Pretty self explanatory, but let's go through each element.

Your office space should be adequate for the type of work you do. For instance, if you create 3D models of proposed buildings for architects, having a tiny table in the corner of your dorm room isn't going to allow you enough space to create these models. Also, if you are a graphic designer and need lots of space for electronics such as a computer and printer(s), you should be in an area that provides for not only space for this equipment but a power source as well.

Something to keep in mind when choosing a work space is how well it functions as a work space. Is it quiet? Well lit? Provides a source of electricity? Does it have the proper furniture for your needs? Is it a space that you see yourself being productive in? If you can't see yourself working in this space, maybe you should look for a better space to do your work in (which I know can be difficult if you live at home with your parents or live in a dorm room).

Once you have your office space chosen, next major element is to make sure it is arranged well. This is when maximizing your space is key. You don't want to push back your chair and you hit the wall behind you; this would soon become a problem. Are all of your tools and required things within arm's reach? Does everything have a place and everything is in its place?

Another thing to keep in mind is if you use this same space for your school work. Chances are you will be doing your school work in the same space. If you use the same space for both your freelancing and your school work, are you prepared to be able to shift between the two when your schedule requires it? Will the presence of one be a distraction for the other?

The final element is to make sure you have everything you need to do your work. If you are a photographer it would be very difficult to do your freelancing without a decent camera. Do you have a well functioning computer with all the necessary software and hardware? Not only do you have industry-specific needs you need to make sure you have but since you are now running a business and you have an office, you need to make sure your office has the necessities: paper, tape, ink, envelopes, stamps, pens, pencils, paperclips, staples, folders, etc.

DIRECTIONS: Is your office in order and ready to serve you well in your new freelancing career? Time to find out! On the next page are three areas of your office that you need to get in order. Read the following questions for each area and make sure each area of your office is ready to tackle your first freelance client with you!

Office space: Have you chosen a great spot where you can set up your office? Is it a space that will help you be productive or could it hinder your productivity? If your first choice for your office space doesn't work, is there another space you can use for your freelancing?

Office arrangement: Is everything within arm's reach? Is there anything in the way that could cause frustration later? Do you have adequate electricity running to your office for

your work? Have you tried several arrangements to make sure you have maximized the space you are in? Have you decided how you will handle working on school work and client work in the same space?

Office supplies: Do you have the necessary supplies needed for your field of freelancing? Is your computer in working order and you have all the required software? Do you have a supply of the essentials such as paper, ink, pens, envelopes, highlighters, etc.?

4.8 Lecture Creating and Keeping Good Records

You may know everything there is to know about your freelancing business and have a good memory but it pays to keep good records of all the different activities you do on the daily basis.

Every business has to keep good records, plain and simple. For a freelancer—especially a student who is very busy most of the year—it is even more important to keep good records. So what type of records should you be keeping?

First and foremost, you need to keep good, detailed records of any money-related activities in your freelance

business. This includes all payments clients have sent you and all expenses for things you have purchased.

I'm very detail-oriented so I keep track of all of my invoices (with numbers, which we will talk about in lesson 5.7), if and when that invoice has been paid, all payments (including date received, from who, payment method such as check or PayPal, and other information as necessary), and I even keep track of the estimates I send out along with their amounts owed.

Keeping good records can help you when you become extremely busy and when it comes to filing your taxes.

Other things to keep track of are really up to you, but are always good to help gauge your success. Such things include how many estimates you have sent out and how many have been accepted (both in numbers and in dollar amounts), time you spend on projects (to help with estimating projects later on), how many hours a day/week/project you are able to bill for compared to how many you have worked (you want your billable hours to increase), etc.

Another aspect of keeping good records is keeping your files organized. You should take care in organizing all of your client and business files. Keeping all your invoices in one folder is great but what happens when you have two or three years of invoices in the same folder? Adding yearly folders inside of an invoice folder helps with that. Also, you should consider dedicating one folder per client too, with multiple projects with the same client getting their own folders as well.

There is no such thing as too much recordkeeping. Well, maybe there is. You should keep detailed records of everything involving your business, but if that recordkeeping starts taking hours and hours out of your day/week, maybe you should think about your system and start simplifying. While these records are great to look back on to help measure your business growth, they shouldn't become time-consuming either.

As a last thought: remember to always keep them up-to-date. We are extremely busy freelancers and students. We can tend to forget things. Spending a couple of hours at the end of every week will save you several headaches and a lot time later on, especially when it comes to paying any taxes or help your cash flow when bills are due.

4.9 Exam Is your office all in order?

Can you feel it yet? You are getting closer and closer to launching your freelancing business!

In this lesson we covered all the aspects you need in order to set up shop. Many of the things we talked about include determining your services, figuring out your ideal client, your portfolio, getting your work and life on a schedule, and how to and why you should maintain good records.

All of these things are grouped together in this lesson because I feel those are the key things you need to go through and complete before you are able to do anything else involving your business—like pricing your services, developing your website, or even start marketing to your target market. These things set you up to be in a great spot to tackle the rest of the things in this book.

DIRECTIONS: Below are statements from different topics we discussed about setting up your freelancing business. Read each one and circle the answer based on things you learned about setting up shop.

TRUE   FALSE

T **F** 1.) Without your portfolio, you cannot freelance.

T **F** 2.) Before you can go searching for your first client, you have to decide what services you can perform first.

T **F** 3.) Since your school schedule is pretty crazy already, you can use your crazy schedule to work on freelancing and homework whenever you want.

T **F** 4.) Some key elements to include in your portfolio are the title of the work, when you completed it and what the size(s) of the work are.

T **F** 5.) An organized and prepared office makes for a happy and productive student freelancer.

(continued on the next page)

T **F** 6.) Getting to know your ideal client means finding out what industry they participate in, their overall attitude toward the services you offer, how knowledgeable are they about your services, and their budget concerns.

T **F** 7.) Doing market research about what types of clients you should market to doesn't apply to freelancers.

T **F** 8.) Portfolios can be put together very quickly so you can move on to other things with freelancing.

T **F** 9.) As a freelancer and business owner, it is important to keep detailed records for things such as income, expenses, invoices, and billable hours.

T **F** 10.) The shotgun approach to marketing works well for freelancers as it increases your chances of landing freelance clients.

SCORING: Did you read between the lines in this lesson? Check your answers against the correct ones below to see how well you know this lesson. If you happen to miss one, go back and review if you have time.

1.) **TRUE.** Harsh, but true. Clients can't hire you if they have no idea what you can do. Your portfolio tells your clients what you are able to do for them. Without a portfolio, your freelancing career can't even get off the ground. *LESSON 4.4*

2.) **TRUE.** Most of your business planning actually can't be done until you determine what you plan to offer to the marketplace. For instance, if you are a designer, what type of design work will you offer? Will you offer only logo design or will you offer logo design in addition to print design? Determining your services will help you find the right clients. *LESSON 4.1*

3.) **FALSE.** You go to school every week on a set schedule, and if you were to have a job you would have to go based on a schedule. Your freelancing shouldn't be any different. Create a schedule that not only dedicates time to everything in your life, but is one that works for you. Just don't forget to actually stick to a set schedule with your freelancing because this is your job! *LESSON 4.6*

4.) **TRUE.** When clients see your portfolio, they need to know the details behind the pieces. These details, along with the medium/media and the client you worked for are details clients look for to better understand how you can help them. Keep it brief, but informative! *LESSON 4.5*

5.) **TRUE.** One of the keys to being successful includes staying organized, and the best place to start is your office area. Make sure your office space is adequate, arranged properly for great productivity, and is supplied with all the needed elements such as a computer, paper and writing instruments. *LESSON 4.7*

6.) **TRUE.** All of these and more are questions you should ask and answer with research when trying to determine your ideal client profile. Getting to know your ideal client allows you to market your services to them. *LESSON 4.3*

7.) **FALSE.** No matter what type of business, you should always do research to determine who will spend their money with you. You need to determining what kind of clients are looking for your services, at what time they are needing them, and how much they can spend. *LESSON 4.2*

8.) **FALSE.** Since your portfolio is the main thing you need for your freelancing and is required when you start marketing yourself, you should take a considerable amount of time preparing your portfolio and making sure it reflects your experience and what you can do for clients. *LESSON 4.4*

9.) **TRUE.** Keeping good records allows you to not have to remember everything all the time. It also makes things such as tax time and evaluating your success much easier, since all the information is already in front of you and you don't have to spend time remembering the details. *LESSON 4.8*

10.) **FALSE.** The shotgun approach to marketing, even when determining who is your ideal client, is never a good approach because it often leads to wasted effort and less return on your efforts. With trying to cater to everyone, you cater to no one. *LESSON 4.2*

GRADE: I'm not looking to see how you did, but you can calculate your score below.

How many you got right: _____ Divided by 10 = _____ x 100 = _____ %

Example: Answered 7 right. 7 / 10 = .7 x 100 = 70%

What is coming up in the next lesson?

For some of you, the next lesson covers all the things you have been waiting for, more specifically, all of the things that involve the color green: moolah, greenbacks, paper, Benjamins, coin, dough, bill, and big ones. Don't know what I am talking about? The next lesson's title will help with that.

Lesson 5

Show Me The Money!

We all like money, right? Well freelancing gives us the opportunity to make some money while we are in school. Often, freelancers can make more money freelancing in the same amount of time they would have spent working at a job like in a restaurant or retail store after their freelancing career is starting to take off. This is often one of the biggest reasons students want to become a freelancer while in school.

This lesson covers the number one topic concerning the starting student freelancer. Things like how much to charge, creating estimates and proposals, budgeting, setting up some way to manage your income, and invoicing clients will be discussed throughout this lesson. Did I mention that you could earn more money for the same amount of time you used to work at your old job?

How Much Should You Charge?

The number one question in freelancing, student status or not, is "how much should I charge?" Well, the best answer is "it depends."

There is no magical dollar amount even though many freelancers wish there was one. As a student, however, that number will be lower than those who are not in school. How come? Often it is because (for the most part) we are less experienced, have less mouths to feed (most of us probably don't have children, spouses, pets), and don't have as many substantial bills such as a mortgage.

All of these weigh in to how much you should charge. There are other factors too such as the type of work you do, the speed at which you do the work, and cost of required software, gear and materials.

In this exercise, I have developed a formula to help you figure out how much you should charge, just like it helped me. It is designed to give you a rough idea on how much to charge in the end, however, you should research and see how your rate below compares to others.

Some common sense also comes into play. For instance, if you came up with $300 an hour and you are a web designer, chances are that rate is a bit high. On the other hand, if

your rate is $20 an hour for photography, that is probably a little on the low end.

DIRECTIONS: Below are several steps that will help you get a rough estimate on how much your hourly fee should be. Go through each section and record the numbers as accurately and precisely as you can. Not sure of a number? Estimate it to the best of your ability to help make sure your hourly fee is as close to accurate as possible.

Current Bills

Take a look at the list below of the most common bills that student freelancers may have (add extras if you need them in the blank lines). Go through them and as accurately as possible estimate the amount each one costs per year. If you are unsure or have a new bill every month, then look at your past three bills, add them up, then multiply by four to get an idea of the amount you anticipate for the year.

Car Loan $_____ per year

Phone Bill $_____ per year

Apartment/House Rent $_____ per year

Electric/Water Bill $_____ per year

Food $_____ per year

Gas/Transportation $_____ per year

Cable TV and/or Internet $_____ per year

Tuition Expenses $_____ per year

School Expenses $_____ per year

_____ $_____ per year

_____ $_____ per year

_____ $_____ per year

_____ $_____ per year

_____ $_____ per year

Total up your yearly personal expenses:
$_____ per year

Start-Up Costs

Next, we need to determine your first year start-up costs you will incur when you start freelancing. Some of these costs include a new computer, upgraded software, special equipment, and other supplies. In the lines below, write out what costs you have associated with starting your freelance business in terms of major one-time expenses. Also be sure to write down the cost of them, too.

_____ $_____

_____ $_____

_____ $_____

_____ $_____

_____ $_____

_____ $_____

_____ $_____

_____ $_____

Total start up costs for your first year:
$_____

Experience Calculation

Finally, we are going to take experience into account. Most freelancing hourly rate calculators don't take into account the experience you have in the field already. So, realistically think about how many years of experience you have in the field of freelancing you wish to enter. This should be the same number you would tell a potential employer if asked how much experience you have.

Years of experience you have: _____ years

Start off with a 1 if you have one year of experience. For every one year of solid experience in your field, add .5 after the first year. For example: I have five years experience in graphic design working for clients and employers. So, I would have an experience calculation of 1+.5+.5+.5+.5 = 3.

First year: 1 + (number of years after 1st year: _____ x .5) = _____. This is your experience calculation we will use later.

You need to take into account the fact you won't be working every single hour of every day. Think about and write down below how many hours per week you intend to work on freelancing and how many weeks a year (remember to give yourself a vacation, holiday, etc). Typically a student freelancer will work an average of twenty hours a week and will do this roughly forty-eight weeks a year.

Hours per week: _____

Operating weeks per year: _____

Putting it all together!

We have all these numbers, but how do they relate to one another to come up with a rough estimate of your hourly rate? Below will take you through the ten steps of the formula so that you can finally calculate your hourly rate!

(1) Yearly Personal Expenses:

_____

(2) Start-Up Costs (write half of that number):

_____

(3) Add lines (1) and (2) together:

_____

(4) Experience Calculation:

_____

(5) Multiply line (3) by line (4):

_____

(6) Multiply line (5) by 1.25 to estimate 25% of taxes owed at the end of each year:

_____

(7) Take your working hours per week and multiply by the number of weeks you will be working to get the number of hours you will be working per year:

_____

(8) Billable hours: Starting at 30% for the first year, add 5% for every year experience afterwards (5 years experience = 30+5+5+5+5=50%). Keep as a percentage:

_____

(9) Multiply line (7) by line (8) to get the average amount of billable hours per year:

_____

(10) Divide line (6) by line (9) to determine your hourly rate per billable hour:

_____

A few notes to keep in mind.

Remember you should compare this number to other freelancers working in the same field with the same amount of experience. While it is not always possible to find other freelancers who do exactly what you do and who are a student as well, getting some other figures to compare yours to will help you iron down your hourly rate.

It is recommended you find at least three other places where there is an average hourly rate for the type of work you do and your experience and/or educational level. You can look at freelancing surveys (we talked about this earlier in the book) to get some rough figures for you to base yours off of. Take three (give or take) averages, add them together, add your hourly rate, then divide by how ever many averages you have plus one (so if you have three averages, you would divide by four).

This gives you an average that takes into account your hourly rate but also the rates of others to see how close you are. While there are many techniques to figure out your ideal hourly rate, averaging data you find with your own hourly rate calculation to get a new average is one of the quickest and easiest ways to get an hourly rate figure you can then base your estimates off of.

Last but not least, go with your gut feeling about your hourly rate. Do you feel like it is too low? Too high? Just right? Often your gut feeling is more accurate than any formula or industry average. Adjust your hourly rate accordingly but still keep in mind that you could end up changing your hourly rate in the future should you figure out it still isn't right.

5.2 Lecture How To Properly Estimate Pricing for Projects

Estimating pricing for projects for the work you do is one of the most challenging things for all freelancers.

With different fields of freelancing comes different ways to estimate projects. Some fields are pretty set in the accepted method that should be charged. For instance, a lawyer or an accountant has a set per-hour fee in which they charge. Other fields, such as event planning or web design may require more of an estimate as to how much the project is going to cost the client when all is said and done and often includes things such as materials and supplies on top of the freelancer's hourly rate.

I will get more into each school of thought and their pros and cons in a second. For now, it is important to discuss no matter which method you choose for estimating projects, it will still come down to how many hours you spend on the project, any associated costs (like printing, web hosting, etc.), taxes, and some sort of percentage to act as a cushion in your estimating.

You need to spend adequate time in estimating how long a particular project is going to take. This is the make-or-break point in your estimating. Estimate too little time and you will either upset the client when you have to charge more or you may be cutting yourself short. On the other hand, estimate too much and the client may feel taken advantage of or you could lose the project all together because your estimate is too high.

It also helps to break down large projects into smaller chunks so that you can more accurately estimate how long each task will take. Most of the time this is where freelancers make mistakes when estimating. They feel the entire group of tasks may take less time than each individual task added up. Splitting up the project so that you can estimate the different milestones will almost certainly allow you to calculate a more accurate estimate.

As always, include any expenses associated with that particular project such as printing costs, purchasing stock imagery, or acquiring web hosting services. These are expenses the client should pay for unless you have some other arrangement for these expenses.

Taxes are a big thing when you are self-employed because you have to pay a lot more of them. I always add a percentage (roughly 25%) to each project to cover for taxes. I store this amount in the savings after I get paid so I have it ready for Uncle Sam come tax time. Be sure, however, to check and see how much taxes you should estimate (this is when a talk with an accountant should come in handy).

Finally, to make sure I have all my bases covered, I add a small percentage (of which I call a cushion) to my projects to cover for estimating mistakes. This is either a small percentage of time when estimating the project and you intend on charging per hour, or to the entire project price including taxes if charging per project.

Charge per hour or per project?

Benefits of charging per hour are you get paid for exactly the amount of hours you work and it's easier to keep track of how long you spend on projects or certain types of projects for future estimating. Downsides include the client being uneasy about the final invoice, clients focus on the money they are paying and not the project itself and punishes you when you work faster.

As you can probably guess, the downsides of charging per hour are the benefits of charging per project; the client no longer focuses on the cost but focuses on the project because they agreed to a price and trust you will charge only that price. Also, if you are able to turn around a project faster, you actually receive a bonus because now your hourly rate for the project just went up (time you spent divided by total amount you charged). Negatives, however, include possibly losing track of how many billable hours you spent working on a project. It is much easier to stop working on something and come back to it when you aren't tracking time you are spending completing the project.

As a final word, it may be best to experiment with both schools-of-thought or even a combination of the two. I started as a charge-by-the-hour freelancer but quickly turned to a charge-by-the-project freelancer when I discovered I was actually getting faster at doing things than I realized. Thus, charging hourly prevented me from making much of income from existing clients and leaving money on the table the client agreed to pay.

5.3 Exercise Creating Proposals and Estimates for Clients

When you get your first freelance project, it can be overwhelming to figure out how to estimate the project and how to share that estimate with your client. This is done through a proposal with an estimate included.

When you land a project from a client, two main things they are going to want to know are what are you going to do for them and how much is it going to cost them. For me and my process, that breaks down into two distinct elements: a proposal and an estimate. Think of your proposals and estimates as tools to persuade your client to hire you; they are marketing tools and should be designed and developed with that in mind.

In short, a proposal is the entire outline of what you are going to do for your client on their project. It outlines what the project is, what needs to be done, what you are going to do, and how long it's going to take (among other things such as some information about you and your experience and skills).

An estimate is how much all of that is going to cost your client, normally stated as a dollar figure (or broken down into different sections with each having a price attached to it). Often, an estimate is included in a proposal, but the estimate is not a proposal as the proposal should be more detailed than just a dollar figure.

The need to have both a proposal and an estimate template is because you will often have various types of projects that will call for different formats in providing estimates for clients. The rule of thumb for me is use estimates for small short jobs, often under a certain dollar amount and less than thirty day projects, and use proposals for much larger projects that require lots of stages and details and often last longer than a month.

Sounds simple enough, right? Well in this exercise we are going to work on creating a "template" for your proposals and estimates. These templates will be used as a framework to help you create your own proposals that can be used on a specific project.

DIRECTIONS: Let's start by creating the framework for your estimates. Estimates should include your client's information (name and contact information), what you will do, how much you will do it for, and how long the estimate is valid for. The best way to use an estimate template in the future is to have a Word document (or any other type of setup; I prefer InDesign) with your branding and information on it, then start organizing the required information within this document. Keep in mind the bulk of the document will be exactly what you will be doing for the client and the pricing, so be sure to leave adequate room for this information.

Also, you should construct your template in a way that if the estimate spans beyond the first page, your template can accommodate it without it looking rough. I often start my estimates and proposals with a cover page that has my contact information and my client's contact information, along with my branding and the title of the project in large

> *Estimates are documents that provide fees and costs of a project, while proposals include an estimate along with providing more in-depth information about the project.*

print. The cover page is often followed by pages that will outline the estimate with only the heading (and sometimes sidebar) of each page being the same throughout.

Next, you will want to work on your proposal template. The proposal template should work much like your estimate template, however it should include specific headings for specific details you should add. What you add in your

proposal template is up to you, but often includes the elements discussed below, plus your estimate.

Some sections of your proposal you may want to consider: a section about you and your professional background, a statement that restates the project in terms of the clients' needs and wants, and what the next steps are to start the project (i.e. stating a deposit and contract is required).

For your starter proposal template, format it more like a school term paper with major headings. While most of the sections of the proposal should be unique from project to project and client to client, there are some sections that will be the same in every proposal (such as your "about me" section).

Thinking of the proposal as a paper will help you better organize the proposal and allow for easier formatting. Paragraphs are a great way to organize content, but keep paragraphs short (often three sentences). When you get down to numbers and dates, use appropriate tables and layouts to best organize this content so your client can clearly understand it.

How Good Are You At Creating Budgets (and Sticking To Them)?

Unless you have money falling from the sky more frequently than it rains, developing a budget will help you keep an eye on your money. How well can you create and manage a budget or multiple budgets?

Unfortunately, we students don't have a good track record or reputation when it comes to managing our money. It's not secret that most students when they graduate college will do so with a heavy burden of debt with a combination of student loans and credit card debt to start paying off soon after graduation. That is why I have said (and will mention several times) "don't use your student loans for freelance expenses!"

Creating and sticking to a budget will help you avoid debt or keep you from going further into debt. The next lesson will talk more in depth about creating budgets and sticking to them. This quiz is designed to see how well you can not only make a budget but keep one as well.

DIRECTIONS: Below are five questions about budgets. Read through them and answer them based on your personal habits and experience.

TRUE FALSE

T **F** 1.) When you go shopping, do you set out a specific budget in which you stick to?

T **F** 2.) Have you ever sat down and made a personal budget for yourself that takes into account your income, monthly bills, money for food and other household items, etc.?

T **F** 3.) When you have made a budget for yourself, have you stuck to it?

T **F** 4.) Do you feel having a budget makes you more money smart?

5.) When operating your freelancing business, do you feel your budget for your freelancing business is just as important as it is for your personal life?

SCORING: Did you answer "yes" to at least four out of the five questions above? If so, you are well-equipped to start creating and sticking to a budget involving both your freelancing life and personal life. Didn't answer "yes" to at least four questions? Well, now is a good time to whip your budget-making muscles into shape.

5.5 Exercise Giving Your Freelancing (and You) A Budget

You think managing your own personal budget is hard? Imagine managing the budgets of both your freelance business and your personal life!

Money management; not very fun sounding but so crucial to the long-term success of your freelance business and even more so with you being a student. As a student freelancer, keeping close tabs on your money such as what comes in, what goes out, and where it goes can help you determine if you are making a profit, what you can afford to spend for certain things, and if you should start saving for a major purchase.

Budgets in your freelance life will work much like they do in your personal life (how well do you keep budgets - according to the previous quiz?). When I first started freelancing, I used much the same setup for my freelancing as I did for my personal finances: I set up a savings fund, emergency fund, and what was left I allocated half for expenses. That has somewhat changed over the years (and yours will too), but essentially they are mostly the same now as they were when I started over five years ago.

When you start working for yourself, there is no reason to go against the grain in terms of the way you already handle your finances. Common sense also comes into play, such as keeping your personal expenses separate from your business and not spending more than you make. Setting up a budget that is easy for you to keep up with and stick to is the key here.

In this exercise, we are going to work on setting up a starting student freelancer budget using many of the same things you currently use in your personal life. We are going to set up your freelancing budget much like setting up "fund" accounts, starting by setting up a couple of must-have funds for your freelancing.

DIRECTIONS: First, you should have a minimum of three different "funds" you should use to allocate part of your income to every month. These three funds should be a taxes fund, emergency fund, and savings fund. Your taxes fund will be for saving a specific amount of your income for your tax bill at the end of the year (so you aren't scrambling for cash to pay Uncle Sam). Your emergency fund will help carry you through any dry months. You should allocate money to this fund when you have money so when you don't have income coming in you can pull from this fund as you need. Finally, your savings fund will help you keep some cash back for major purchases or any other major expenses or needs, such as a new computer, equipment repairs, etc.

Figure out exactly how much of your paycheck should go to your taxes, emergency, and savings funds. Between these three accounts, I would put no more than 40% total of your income into these funds; you have to eat and pay your personal bills with what is left!

The remainder of your income can then be split into other needs, such as a paycheck and your business expenses. This will vary from freelancer to freelancer, so figure out what best works for you as to how much you should pay yourself and what you should leave behind to pay your freelance bills. What you pay yourself is considered your personal income and can be split up into a budget very similar to the one above for your freelancing.

You may find yourself having to work with the percentages or amounts to get everything to work out correctly and/or you may have to make changes to it as time goes on and with practice. I review my budgets at the beginning of every year to make sure they are working well for me with my changing situations.

As long as you are not spending more than you are making, you are able to pay your taxes on time and in full, you are able to put money away for a rainy day, and pay yourself to take care of your needs, then your budget is a success!

Staying Out of Debt.

With any serious budget, one of the goals is to work toward getting and staying out of debt. While you are working on your freelance business, don't put yourself into debt just to get things moving. You may need to purchase new equipment or things, but plan out these purchases so that you don't buy so much that your freelancing can't pay for it. Also, don't use your student loans for business expenses either (sound familiar?).

5.6 Exercise Setting Up Your Money Management System

You don't need fancy software to manage your cash flow. Doing things you already do and using software you already use will help you to stay on top of what money you have made and what invoices haven't been paid.

Everyone who knows me knows that I'm very detail-oriented. So much so that after trying out tons and tons of different kinds accounting and money management applications, I came up empty-handed, hours wasted, and with nothing that worked for me.

It wasn't soon after that when I discovered that I didn't have to have any of the software others were using. Since I was detailed in everything I did and had a very specific way I wanted to handle things, I decided to do what worked for me and what I was already comfortable with.

Before I discuss the different options for your money management system and getting started creating your own, let me start off by saying that you should focus on what you naturally do already in your life, meaning if you are a wiz at Excel, use Excel; if you like to keep everything down on paper, keep it on paper (but have some way to back it up). There is no need to go against what you already do when you start freelancing (haven't I said this before?).

There are several different ways to create your own money management system. You could keep things detailed on paper using graph paper or even buy special finance books. For those of you skilled in spreadsheet programs, that would be a great place to create your system (that is how I have created mine). If you don't really have any set way currently, it is perfectly OK to do some Googling and find different apps and services that can do it all for you.

Whichever method you choose, make sure you have the basics covered. At the bare minimum you will want to keep track of invoices (if they are paid, if they are late, who they were to, what was it for), payments (from who, amount, yearly running total), expenses (what did you buy, what was it for, is it tax-deductible), and your business-only bank accounts (basically a check register).

Creating your money management system is very easy; you just need to pick which method you want to use (paper, spreadsheet, app, etc.) and what things you want to keep track of. Also, as a note of caution: your money management system is only as good as you make it and maintain it. It is not a one time set-up and let it run. You will always have to make sure you are entering in the right information and in a timely fashion.

DIRECTIONS: Now it is time to develop your money management system! Since it doesn't take much to create one, let's get yours started and ready for when you start making that hard-earned freelance money.

First, review the different methods of record keeping we discussed above. Are you used to keeping things in order on paper, do you know how to use a spreadsheet program, or would you prefer to start looking for an already created money management system online or as an application?

Write down what method(s) you want to try. Don't be afraid to try out more than just one at the same time to see which you like better.

_____

_____

_____

_____

_____

_____

Next, in the method(s) that you have chosen, make sure it has the basics: invoices, payments, expenses, and your bank account register. For those of you doing this on paper and/or spreadsheet programs, this is just as easy as setting up one page for each of those mentioned with those sheets having columns for information needed such as date, amount, running totals, and what they were for. For those of you looking to use an application or service, check to see if these things exist. If they don't, you may need to keep looking to find one that works for you.

Once you have organized your money management system and have all of the necessary items, you are ready to move on to what will start bringing you money to put into your system: invoices.

5.7 Lecture Invoicing Clients

Besides actually doing the work, how else are you going to make money?

You can't make money unless you invoice your clients. For those unfamiliar with the term "invoice," it simply means sending a bill. In order to get paid for all of your hard work on a project, you have to invoice your clients.

In this lecture I'm going to break down the process of invoicing a client. Depending on how you set your business up, more than likely you will receive a deposit from a client in order to start work (or at least I hope you will get a deposit before you begin work). While most freelancers are split on this idea, invoicing for a deposit can be up to you. I invoice for deposits simply because it helps me keep records. Also, it is a signal to the client that you are ready to start their project (and it doesn't hurt to put a little pressure on your client to quickly pay the invoice—allowing you to start sooner).

So what things should you include on your invoice? These things are absolutely required on any invoice from any business: your name (or business name), phone number, and address; client's name and address; invoice number (each invoice gets its own number in order similar to checks in your checkbook); invoice date; invoice due date; what

services were rendered or a description of what the invoice is for; the amount due; and how the client can pay you (check, PayPal, credit card, etc.). Those are the absolute must-haves.

Other items you could include on your invoice are: your business logo, payment terms, a brief "thank you" message, project number, previous payments received, payment stub, and any "office only" lines (I have a few on mine that include payment received, payment method, and check number all on the stub, so when I get the stub back I can fill it in).

The next important thing is to make sure you lay out your invoice in a professional and easy-to-understand manner. Don't make your clients work to see how much they owe, when it is due, or what the invoice was for. With that in mind, a quick Google search for "invoice templates" will help steer you in the right direction when you start working on your invoice template.

When you start looking for invoice templates, you will see the invoice number is often at the top, and the amount due is often at the bottom. It is best not to break from convention on something like your invoice, but don't be afraid to lay it out differently or add additional elements based on your own needs. Designing your own invoice template to match your logo and your visual identity will help show you as being even more professional and give clients peace of mind when working with you.

5.8 Lecture Accounting Practices for Freelancers

Even though you are running your own freelance business and can manage the office end of things any way you want, there are some general things that will help you and your accountant come tax time.

Closely related to taxes, the way you keep records and file taxes is very important and requires the help of an accountant. An accountant is going to be able to help you with your expenses, federal and local taxes, and keeping clean accounting records.

You will either be working on a cash accounting system (you count income when you receive it) or an accrual accounting system (you count income when you bill for it). Most freelancers work on a cash accounting system. An accountant will help you set up how to keep your records based on one of these two systems.

Most freelancers will work on the cash accounting system which means you make money when it is actually in your hands (not when you invoice for it). This is often easier to manage and is more accurate for freelancers, especially student freelancers.

To help your accountant, make sure you keep accurate records of your income, expenses, and other particulars. You don't need any fancy accounting software such as Quickbooks. If you manage your stuff in a spreadsheet, that should be good enough for an accountant for the low volume of transactions you will have (after all, you aren't a grocery store with thousands of transactions a day).

You should always keep a good record of all of your invoices (who you sent them to, if they were paid, etc.), your expenses relating to your business (what you bought, how much you spent, what was it for, etc.), and other money related aspects of your business such as payment fees charged to you for accepting PayPal or credit card payments, cashing a check, etc.

Keeping all this information in an organized manner and keeping it up to date allows for your accountant to better handle your taxes when it comes time to file. As an incentive, remember that every expense you record could help lower your tax bill!

5.9 Exam Are you ready to make some serious moolah?

Think you know all about the money side of freelancing? Let's test your knowledge with the quiz below!

We covered quite a bit of ground here, all involving making money. Everything from figuring out what to charge to creating estimates, invoicing clients to managing payments. Getting things ready and organized ahead of time will help when things start getting busier and you need to keep track of your income. There were many things covered in this lesson, so did you learn a lot? In the exam that follows, test your knowledge about all the things we talked about where it comes to money and being a student freelancer.

DIRECTIONS: Below are ten statements about gaining and managing money as a student freelancer. Answer "true" or "false" based on what you learned about freelancing moolah.

TRUE   FALSE

T **F** 1.) Coming up with an estimate for clients involves estimating your time then multiplying by your hourly rate.

T **F** 2.) Your money management system will help you keep track of invoices, payments, and expenses.

T **F** 3.) It's OK if you don't keep detailed records; that is why you hire an accountant.

(continued on the next page)

T F 4.) Invoices are documents clients send you with their payments.

T F 5.) The difference between a proposal and an estimate is that an estimate involves mainly the fees associated with the project while a proposal includes an estimate along with more specific details relating to the project.

T F 6.) Start-up costs are only the costs you incur before you start freelancing.

T F 7.) While you should develop a budget to follow in your personal life, your freelance business can operate without a budget.

T F 8.) When coming up with your rate, the three major factors you should include are: your current bills, start-up costs, and your experience.

T F 9.) Creating your freelance budget involves creating one fund for taxes, while splitting the remaining income however you would like.

T F 10.) An invoice often includes your business name and/or logo, the amount owed, payment terms, the client's information such as their address, the date of the invoice, and the due date.

SCORING: Find out which ones you got right by comparing the answers below with your selections above and lesson numbers to review the ones you missed.

1.) **FALSE.** There are other elements to consider when coming up with an estimate for a client such as project-specific expenses, taxes and administration costs. Not including these could hurt your income. *LESSON 5.2*

2.) **TRUE.** Using either paper or a spreadsheet, keeping track of invoices will let you see who you have invoiced and what is outstanding. Keeping track of payments will make it easier to see your yearly income. Finally, tracking expenses will help you make deductions at tax time. *LESSON 5.6*

3.) **FALSE.** You will make your accountant's job harder if they have to sort through your lack of records to do things such as calculate and file your taxes. Keeping good records makes it easier and could even save you money. *LESSON 5.8*

4.) **FALSE.** You're actually the one that sends invoices to clients requesting payment for services rendered. If you don't send an invoice that outlines what you have done for them, you may not get paid for your work. *LESSON 5.7*

5.) **TRUE.** Estimates are really only concerned with outlining fees and costs for the project. Proposals on the other hand outline everything in the estimate and things like a general understanding of the client project, a project time line, and information about you and your business. *LESSON 5.3*

6.) **FALSE.** While the bulk of start-up costs come before you can even start freelancing, throughout the first year of your freelancing you will incur other start-up costs like one time purchases such as software and materials. *LESSON 5.1*

7.) **FALSE.** You will need to develop and stick to a budget in your freelance business just like you do in your personal life. Thankfully, you can make your freelance budget work similarly to your personal budget. *LESSON 5.5*

8.) **TRUE.** There is no magic formula for calculating your rate, however, these are the major things you should consider. While both current bills and start-up costs

are things that freelancers must think about, student freelancers must evaluate their experience a bit differently when determining their rate. *LESSON 5.1*

9.) **FALSE.** Your freelancing budget should have at least three funds: tax, emergency and savings fund. Your tax fund allows for putting money back for taxes, your emergency fund helps you through slow times, and your savings fund helps you make large purchases. *LESSON 5.5*

10.) **TRUE.** In addition to those mentioned, other things to include on your invoice are invoice number, services rendered and how they can send you payment. *LESSON 5.7*

GRADE: Compute your grade using the formula below.

How many you got right: _____ Divided by 10 = _____
x 100 = _____ %

Example: Answered 8 right. 8 / 10 = .8 x 100 = 80%

What's going to happen next?

In the next lesson we are going to get everything ready for opening day including developing your look, your website, and promoting yourself before you finally cut the ribbon on your grand opening! Join me in the next lesson!

Lesson 6

Getting Ready to Launch

We have done a lot of work to get to this point. We have worked on our business plan, figured out who our target market is, determined the services we are going to offer, and how much we are going to charge. We have also talked about researching the industry, building a financial safety net, taxes, and how to manage your income.

With all of this work done, you are very close to launching your new freelance business! There are just a few more things that have to be done before you can finally start! In this lesson we will develop your identity, work on your website, double check everything, and start promotion. Finally, we will end with launching your freelance business!

6.1 Exercise Developing Your Identity

What is your business going to look like to prospective clients? How will they recognize you?

The designer in me is screaming out "it's time for a logo!" Since you are right there, almost ready to launch your freelance business, it is now time for the fun stuff! You worked on getting your business name, what services you are going to offer and all of that squared away, now it's time for the icing on the cake!

The term "identity" can be defined in many different ways, but in terms of your freelancing business it is the way you are going to look. This means coming up with a logo, website, marketing materials, etc. All these things together will develop your identity in the eyes of the marketplace and prospective clients.

One of the drawbacks of being a student freelancer is you may not have as much experience or may not be on the same level as other freelancers in your field. One of the ways to counteract this and make it less of an impact is to develop a solid visual professional presence. Professional businesses have a solid way in which they look and present themselves. Your logo is the start of making that professional look for your business.

Since we will talk about your website and other materials throughout the rest of this lesson, in this section we are going to focus on your logo. Since there are a variety of different types of student freelancers reading this book, I am going to be as broad as possible in this section.

It is time to develop your logo! Fun, awesome, and amazing things are about to happen when you launch your freelancing business, all of which means you need to look good and professional from day one.

DIRECTIONS: With your business name in hand, it is time to start thinking about and developing your logo. Since there are a variety of people reading this book, read through and select one of the following courses of action that best describes your situation.

Of course, if you are a designer, you should really design your own logo. Matter of fact, you should design everything involving your business!

If you are not a designer and not creative at all, you should seek the help of someone who is creative. Find a fellow classmate who is a designer and see if they would be willing to help you create a logo or even create one for you. It's a win-win: you can use it for your business and they can use it for their portfolio. Depending on the nature of the agreement, you may have to pay them a little bit to do the work or you may get away with just buying them lunch.

If you are in a field that doesn't have many creative types around, seek professional help with your logo from a designer. This option will more than likely cost you money, but if it helps you stand out and look more professional, it is an investment worth investing for your new student freelancing career.

So what is your course of action? Are you going to develop your own logo, hire someone to do it, or find a classmate who is willing to create one for you? If someone else is going to develop the logo for you, do you have that person chosen already? Who are they?

6.2 Lecture Your Website

In today's world, a website is no longer a luxury, but a necessity. We live in a digital world and our freelancing should live in it too.

I would have to say that if I had to pick one single thing that every freelancer should have no matter what, that one thing would be a website. More specifically, every freelancer should have a website with information about them, their work, and what they can be hired to do.

If you haven't already thought about your website, let me push you into reality. While you are thinking about starting freelancing while in school, you should spend most of your time getting your website started and ready for clients to see your work and see what you can do for them.

There is so much information that can go on your site, but it is important to keep your website brief and provide the right information. Below I am going to outline exactly what you need, from start to finish, when it comes to getting your website and what you should have on your website.

First off, if you don't already have these things, you should look for an available domain name (such as google.com) and a hosting provider. Every single website must have these two things. Your domain name acts as an address to your website, where hosting is where your website lives.

While you are working on these things, it doesn't hurt to develop your own email address at your domain—such as amber@amberturner.com—as your custom email address always looks more professional.

Next is to start planning out your website! There is a ton of information you can have on your website, but it is possible not all of it is needed. You want to give your potential clients adequate information about what you do and your work but not so much that they feel overwhelmed. Let's cover the big things you may want to have on your website.

Portfolio

Your clients are hiring you to produce some sort of creative piece and they are going to want to see what you have done in the past. For most student freelancers, your portfolio is going to be the bulk of your site.

We discussed portfolios back in lesson four so you should have all of your work ready to format for your website. Depending on the type of freelancing you do, you should limit your portfolio to your best pieces and the pieces that showcase the type of work you want to be hired to do.

Services

Also in lesson four, we talked about what your services should be and organized your services so that clients understand what they can hire you for. You will want to put this on your website as well in easy-to-understand terms for your client. Also, keep it short and sweet. Your clients are very busy people and don't want to read a book to find out about your services (plus you are a busy college student and I'm sure you don't want to spend your entire day writing!).

Contact Information

In order for clients to be able to hire you, they should be able to contact you! Such contact information that you should have includes your phone number and email address. You can also include your Twitter handle, Facebook page, and your Skype username.

Another item you will want to have on your site is a contact form. This is an easy, no hassle way for clients to contact you immediately. A simple form will do, such as one that asks for the client's name, phone number, email address, and asks them to write about why they are contacting you.

About You

Often, freelancers will include information on their site about themselves. As students, we could get carried away in talking about ourselves, but if you want to include some information about yourself on your site, you need to remember to keep it short and professional.

The main reason to have some information about yourself on your site is it makes you more personable and more approachable. Clients can read about you and get to know you before they even start talking to you.

Blog

Finally, freelancers are starting to add blogs to their sites to write about various topics in their field of freelancing. This is a great way to show your knowledge and skills in another way other than your portfolio. A blog is a constantly updated part of your site that shares this knowledge.

I do caution freelancers who want to include a blog on their site. While it is a great feature to have as it can help educate clients and show that you are keeping up with your site, the downside to that is if you don't keep up with your site. Having a blog on your site you don't update is the quickest way to make your website become stale. Unless you plan to have tons of time to keep a blog running, you may want to reconsider adding this feature to your website.

6.3 Exercise Getting Your Website Ready for Prime Time

Now that we talked about websites for student freelancers, it is time to get yours ready for the big launch!

We just finished discussing the importance of having a website as a student freelancer and what all your website should have. Everything from your portfolio to your contact information, even to the possibility of a blog are all great things to have on your website. But what things are best suited for you and your field of freelancing?

In this exercise we are going to figure out exactly what you need on your website, write the various copy (or wording) you will use on your site and finally put it all together on your website.

DIRECTIONS: Now is the time to get your website up and running, but before we can do that we need to plan out what should be on your website.

Reviewing the last lecture, figure out the major pieces you want on your website. These pieces could be your portfolio, about page, and contact page. We discussed several pieces of your website but not all of them may be best suited for you. Below, write down what pieces of information you want on your website:

_____

_____

_____

_____

_____

_____

_____

_____

_____

_____

Now that we have a good idea of what you want on your website, take some time to write out everything that should go on your site. For instance, for your portfolio write out titles, descriptions, and any other important information you want on the site. If you are including an "about me" page, be sure to write out your bio and polish it so it flows well, sounds professional, and is free of spelling mistakes and grammatical errors.

You should plan out all of the copy ahead of time so that it is something you don't just add to your site with plans to change it later and then never change it. Also, it allows you to focus on the site itself instead of its content and often allows you to produce a more professional site.

Finally, it's time to make your site and add all of your content. If you already have a website, then you can make changes to your site and add your new content to get your site ready for your launch.

If you don't have a website already, you should purchase your domain name and hosting. Next, you should either partner with a web designer, find a web designer friend, or look into installing WordPress and using one of the many free themes in order to get your website going. There are many free resources in getting your website going, many of which are listed in the back of this book.

The most important thing in this exercise is to have your website completely ready to go. How much work you have to do depends on where you are on your website coming into this exercise. Take the tips and information shared in this exercise and in the previous lecture, along with online resources to get your website in tip-top shape.

6.4 Quiz Double Check Everything

That big day is getting closer and closer! Do you have everything ready to start your freelancing career?

Well, you have made it this far. You've done all the research, planning, and work you needed to do to get your freelance business off the ground. Everything from creating a business plan to setting up budgets, getting your website up and running to getting your office organized, and even have a mentor ready to help you when you need it.

On the next page are twenty questions all relating to topics and exercises we have talked about so far in this book. Since you are so close to launching and telling the world about your new business, let's make sure you have everything ready and all your bases are covered!

DIRECTIONS: So are you ready to start your freelancing career as a student? Answer the following questions relating to things we have talked about so far. Have you completed everything and ready to get your freelancing business off the ground?

YES   NO

Y **N**   1.) Did you determine if you have at least fifteen hours a week you can dedicate to your freelancing career?

Y **N**   2.) Did you write down all your ideas back in lesson two? Did you read and do some research to help generate even more ideas?

Y **N**   3.) Did you take a look through at least one of the industry reports I mentioned? Did you read through them and find stats and information that could help you make decisions later on?

Y **N**   4.) Do you have a mentor in place, someone whom you feel comfortable talking to and is willing to help you when needed?

Y **N**   5.) Did you take the appropriate steps to make sure you have an adequate financial safety net that includes up to six months of your expenses?

Y **N**   6.) Did you develop a working business plan, and have you been tweaking and working on it as you progress through this book?

Y **N**   7.) Did you develop a time line to help keep yourself on track and make sure you get everything done by your grand opening (as discussed in lesson 2.9)?

Y **N**   8.) Personal name or business name? Have you picked which one you are going to go with? Have you made the big decision on what you are going to name your freelancing?

Y **N**   9.) Have you worked on a working contract yet, one you can take to a lawyer to get reviewed?

Y **N** 10.) What are your clients going to hire you to do? We talked about how to determine your services. Do you have a nice list of services you are going to offer?

Y **N** 11.) Have you figured out who your potential clients are? Do you know how you will market to them?

Y **N** 12.) Have you pulled together your best work and are ready to show them to potential clients?

Y **N** 13.) Have you picked your office, arranged it so that it's functional, and bought necessary office supplies?

Y **N** 14.) Are you a good record keeper? Have you figured out how you will keep good records for things such as invoices, payments and clients?

Y **N** 15.) Have you determined what your freelancing rates will be and how you will charge your clients?

Y **N** 16.) Do you have your estimate and proposal templates ready to go for your very first client prospect? Do they have your branding and information on them as well?

Y **N** 17.) Did you take the budget quiz back in lesson five? Have you set up your own budget for your freelance business and your life as a student?

Y **N** 18.) Is your money management system ready for your first day of freelancing? No matter if it is on paper or in a spreadsheet, is it set up and ready?

Y **N** 19.) Is your invoicing system and template ready for sending to clients? Do you have all of the required elements of an invoice included in your template?

Y **N** 20.) Have you gotten your website domain name and hosting? Is your website up and running for all to see?

Haven't done something yet?

Time is ticking! Haven't done something that is in the quiz on the last page (meaning that you had to circle "no" instead of "yes")? Now is a great time to make a list of those things and tackle them before moving on. The big launch is quickly approaching, so it is time to get everything done so you can relax and enjoy the launch of your business, without feeling stressed!

DIRECTIONS: Below are some lines you can use to create a quick to do list of things you marked "no" to on the last two pages. Write out what you still need to do and set a deadline on when you will get those things done. If you are in the process of getting something done (for instance, you have a meeting with an accountant but that meeting hasn't happened yet), write down that information as well. This is to help keep you organized!

6.5 Exercise Promoting Your Freelancing Before the Big Launch

You are almost there! While it would be so easy to just open your doors, you aren't quite there yet. However, that doesn't mean that you can't start promoting yourself so that your grand opening is even more fruitful.

One of the things I wish I'd done when I started freelancing (and was able to do when I relaunched my business) was promote myself before I launched my business. The reason is because it can be quite discouraging to put in all of this work into launching your business and then you finally launch your business only to find little to no response.

Why not generate some of that response early? For student freelancers, you can start promoting yourself right before you officially launch your business. I am sure you are wondering how you can do this without having actually launched. No worries; in this lesson we are going to talk about a few ways you can start promoting your freelancing before you launch your business!

DIRECTIONS: Let's talk about three different things you can do right now to promote yourself even before you officially launch your freelancing business as a student.

I'm sure by now you have already talked to friends and family about your new freelancing endeavor, so you can use that to your advantage. When you talk to friends and

family, talk to them about your business and make them excited for you can help. When you can make them excited they could start telling their friends and family who may be interested in your services. By the time this word of mouth takes off, you will have opened your doors and are ready to start accepting clients.

You can take talking with your friends and family to the next level by handing out business cards to those you talk to. Be sure to hand them a minimum of three business cards: one to keep and two to give away. Encourage them to give the cards to those who may be interested in the services you offer.

Finally, use social media to your advantage. If you already have a Facebook page for your business, you can start posting teaser information and information about your services. Use Twitter to share information about you and what you can do. You can also promote your launch by posting statuses about how many days are left until you can start accepting clients.

6.6 Exercise Launching Your Freelance Business

All that hard work and planning has hopefully prepared you to tell the world you are a freelancer!

Now that all of your planning is done and you are ready to rock and roll, it is time to put all of that planning to the test by launching your freelancing business!

While there is no set way on how to launch your freelance business, there are some things that should be ready to go and all you have to do is pull the trigger. For instance, you should have a website up and ready to go, so all you need to do is launch it!

DIRECTIONS: In this exercise, go through all of your planning in the last lesson and start launching each

necessary thing. For instance, you may have your website ready to launch, business cards ready to hand out, Twitter and Facebook ready to activate, etc. Tell the world about what you are doing and let them know you are now accepting projects!

I have created some lines for you to write down what items you need to launch. Once you have launched and/or activated them, simply mark them out. Use the lines as a to do list to make sure all your bases are covered!

_____

_____

_____

_____

_____

_____

_____

_____

_____

_____

Congrats! You are now officially a student freelancer! Did you do everything as planned in the first half of this book?

We covered quite a bit of information in this lesson as we were on the last stretch before launching our freelancing business. Everything from developing an identity, getting your website together, and finally launching your freelancing business are all the last things to do before you start working with clients and growing your new freelance business all while you are still in school! Let's review all the things we talked about with a quick quiz before moving on to the next phase of your business: growth!

DIRECTIONS: Read the statements below and answer "true" or "false" based on what you learned about getting ready to launch your freelancing business.

TRUE   FALSE

T **F**   1.) It is recommended that every student freelancer have a blog on their website.

T **F**   2.) Developing a solid visual professional presence with a logo and marketing materials helps student freelancers gain credibility with potential clients.

T **F**   3.) Once you have done everything on your freelance business launch list, you are ready to start taking clients!

T **F**   4.) Information about you on your website can be one of the biggest parts of your website.

T **F**   5.) Your website should be ready to go and fully operational when you launch your freelancing business.

T **F**   6.) Information on your website should be brief, complete, and relative to your freelancing.

T **F**   7.) You should start promoting yourself to potential clients only after you have officially opened your doors.

(continued on the next page)

T **F** 8.) Coming up with a launch checklist and making sure you have everything in order is highly recommended.

T **F** 9.) All you need to get your website going is an available domain name (i.e. studentsthatfreelance.com).

T **F** 10.) Student freelancers can use their extensive knowledge of social media when promoting themselves.

SCORING: Below are the answers so that you can compare them to your selections above. There are lesson numbers for each one so you can go back and review.

1.) **FALSE.** While there are other sections that should be on your website such as your portfolio, ways to contact you, and information about you, not every student freelancer should have a blog on their site. Only if you intend to stay on top of constantly adding new content to your blog should you consider adding one. *LESSON 6.2*

2.) **TRUE.** When student freelancers present themselves as a business with professional materials such as a logo, website and marketing materials, clients will take them more seriously than if these materials have been quickly put together without care or do not exist at all. *LESSON 6.1*

3.) **TRUE.** Hopefully you've made a checklist of all the things you need to do on opening day. If you have everything in order and ready to go, work your way through this checklist to officially start freelancing! *LESSON 6.6*

4.) **FALSE.** When you share information about you, keep it brief and professional. Chances are if you do this it will be one of the smallest parts of your website. The largest part of your website should be your portfolio. *LESSON 6.3*

5.) **TRUE.** We spent significant time on getting your site up and running because as soon as you start marketing yourself and telling people you are available for hire, they will want to see your website. *LESSON 6.3*

6.) **TRUE.** With so much information you can put on your website, the content needs to not only gain your clients attention but be respectful of your client's time by staying brief, giving them all the information they need, and keeping it professional and related to your specific type of freelancing. *LESSON 6.2*

7.) **FALSE.** Your new freelancing business will take off much faster if you start promoting yourself a couple of weeks before your official launch date. It takes a while for marketing efforts to become fruitful, so getting a head start can benefit you and help you from becoming discouraged in the beginning. *LESSON 6.5*

8.) **TRUE.** You don't want to get so excited that you miss something when it comes to launching your business. It is worth taking a few extra moments to create and run through a checklist (like the one we provided) so that you can tie up loose ends. *LESSON 6.4*

9.) **FALSE.** Not only do you need to purchase an available domain name, you also need to purchase hosting as well. Your website can't be seen by anyone unless there is a place to store it which is what hosting will do. Your domain name points people to your website on your server. *LESSON 6.2*

10.) **TRUE.** Often the largest part of our network exists in the social media networks we participate in. Use this to your advantage when you start promoting your new freelancing business. *LESSON 6.5*

GRADE: Hoping for a high score? The formula below will help you calculate your grade on this lesson's exam.

How many you got right: _____ Divided by 10 = _____ x 100 = _____ %

Example: Answered 10 right. 10 / 10 = 1 x 100 = 100%

What is in store for the next lesson?

First of all, congrats on making it this far through the book! It has been a great journey in planning your new freelancing business and you have finally launched your business you have been working very hard on!

The first part of this book was all about planning your business launch, everything from naming your freelance business, getting contracts together, figuring out your pricing and services, getting your website up and going with your portfolio to finally launching your business.

Now that you are officially a self-employed student doing the things you love, the next phase is making your business grow! We are transitioning here from the beginning stages of your business before you launch to running your business after the launch.

Businesses succeed when they grow, so in the next lesson we are going to talk about marketing your new freelancing business, such as developing a marketing plan, updating your website, and using social media and your network to help you get your first client. I'll see you in the next lesson!

Lesson 7

Scream From The Rooftops (Marketing)

Now that you have your freelance business up and running, it's time to start promoting yourself! Marketing as a student freelancer isn't all it is cracked up to be and requires learning a few new things paired with a lot of hard work.

In this lesson we are going to talk about several aspects of marketing for student freelancers, such as what marketing is, developing a marketing plan, fine-tuning your website, different types of marketing, developing your network, and finally, discuss how you can find your first client.

7.1 Lecture An Overview of Marketing for Freelancers

Now that the wheels are turning on your freelance business, you should start marketing yourself to anyone who could use your services.

Marketing is hard work. Trust me, I got a degree in it. It isn't an exact science and it definitely is much harder to do as a freelancer than it is for a corporation, especially if you are a student and haven't had much experience working for a service-based business in the past.

Any discussion about marketing warrants a few key points. Most freelancers, if not all of them, when they first start freelancing feel they should market themselves to everyone. This is simply a waste of time and what most people in the marketing world call the "shotgun" approach to marketing. They throw out their marketing messages to anyone and everyone they can.

Not only does the message get to people who aren't looking for your services, it starts to make you look desperate and unprofessional as you didn't take the time to figure out exactly who needs your services and where they are located. Avoid standing on the rooftop screaming to everyone you are a freelancer and you are looking for work because it just isn't going to bring home the bacon.

So who should you target and where can you find them? This all depends on the type of freelancer you are. If you are a wedding photographer, chances are you will want to go to bridal trade shows, hook up with wedding and event planners, and talk to people to see if they know of anyone who recently got engaged and needs a photographer for their wedding.

If you are a writer, contact blogs online that feature content in the topics you are most interested in. For designers, small businesses are often gold mines as they don't have anyone internally doing their design work and could greatly benefit from having someone with an eye for design working on their materials and other needed items.

Another key point to remember is not every means of marketing is going to be fruitful. While everything is worth trying to see if it works for you, some avenues are just not going to work out. For instance, putting an ad in the paper for copywriting work will likely go nowhere, as those who are looking for that type of work are not going to pick up a newspaper to look for copywriters. Now, they may pick up a phone book so you could put an ad in there, but who uses a phone book much anymore?

Social media is one of those outlets that tends to be one that works in some form or fashion for every type of freelancer. No freelancer, especially student freelancers, should ignore the power of word-of-mouth and social media has that exact power. Other avenues of marketing include your website (which helps you be found on Google and other search engines), business cards, becoming friends with other freelancers in related fields, attending business group meetings in your city (such as chamber of commerce brunches), and word-of-mouth.

Keep in mind your budget for marketing. Even though one avenue may seem really great, you can't put all of your eggs in one basket and put all of your budget for marketing toward that one avenue. I'm always wanting to stretch my dollar as far as it can go, so I break it up and try a few things at the same time instead of one thing all the way.

Another related point is that every type of marketing requires a test period, where a limited amount of funds and energy are put toward that media in order to see if it is a viable option. You may discover social media is just not working for you after a test period. If you were to have all of your budget toward social media, your budget would be blown. However, if you invested in social media, your website, and business cards, only part of your marketing efforts were wasted and you can take the social media budget and try a different media.

Now, how long a test period depends on the media you plan to use. Take for example direct mail marketing. A reasonable test period for this is probably six months. However, a reasonable test period for something as quick as Google Adwords may be shorter, like three months.

Marketing is a lot of trial and error, but once you are able to figure out just the right combination of media that works best for you (which takes roughly a year or two from my experience), you will be able to exploit those and use them to your advantage while spending less and less for those avenues. As long as you stay organized and record the results of any marketing you do, you should be able to quickly determine what is working and what is not before you spend any more money on something that just isn't producing the results you are looking for.

In the next section, we'll take all of these tips and come up with a rough marketing plan in which you can start testing some marketing media to see what works best for you.

Until you know what works for you, you have to test the waters with different types of marketing strategies and compare them.

With marketing being such a tricky thing to deal with, often freelancers have to try a couple of things to see what works best. Many freelancers do this during their first year but after their first year they start to see what works and are able to run with what works.

So now you know who your target market is and where they can be found, the next step is to figure out what media is associated where both of these overlap. Taking our example, those planning a wedding are more tuned in to anything bridal: magazines, TV shows, bridal trade shows, other friends and family who are recently married, and especially wedding websites online.

Make a list of the media often used by your target market or in the places in which your target market can be found. A little research may be necessary to compile a comprehensive list. It is also notable to write down any way that you discover how your target market interacts with these media. Do they use it a lot? A little? What are they looking for? Write your results in the blanks below.

_____

_____

_____

_____

Next step is pick three of the above you feel would produce the best results in terms of marketing. Use a highlighter or circle them above. These three items are going to be tested to see how fruitful they are when it comes to marketing your services.

DIRECTIONS: Develop a rough plan for each of the media you circled/highlighted above. How often are you going to send marketing messages? How much money are you going to dedicate to it? How are you going to measure its success (or failure)? For how long are you going to test it

(I suggest a minimum of three months)? Are you willing to stop it sooner if it is not working out? Answer all of these questions and provide as much detail for each of the three media you selected in order to develop a plan for how to market your freelance business. Use the areas below to organize your ideas.

1.) _____
_____
_____
_____
_____

2.) _____
_____
_____
_____
_____

3.) _____
_____
_____
_____
_____

All that is left is to pull the trigger! Put those plans above into action and start recording the results. If some or all are producing the results you want, continue them! However, if they aren't working out, look back at where your target market hangs out and pick another one to try out.

Keep doing the same thing until you come up with three solid marketing avenues that are working well for you.

7.3 Exercise Fine-Tuning and Updating Your Website

You've been in business for a little bit now and have learned a thing or two about what is working and what isn't. Since your launch, certain things have probably taken a back seat such as your website. It's time to fine tune your website to make it really work for you.

With all of your marketing goals and efforts we discussed in the last two parts of this lesson, your biggest marketing tool is your website. You probably haven't had a chance to update it since your launch (have you?).

It's really good to make it a habit to look at your website as your business grows and make sure everything is still working the way you would like for it to. Are your clients finding you by your website? Is it still functioning well (meaning nothing is broken, your contact form is still working)? Is your portfolio up-to-date?

Even if you haven't had the chance to work with a client or finish a client project yet, it doesn't hurt to do some fine-tuning to your website. You probably haven't looked at it in a while and with anything a fresh look at a project can reveal things you need to do.

No matter how long ago it was when you became a student freelancer, it's a great time to look at your website to see what things you can improve on or change.

DIRECTIONS: Get out a piece of paper and take a good look through your website to see if there is anything you would like to improve. At this stage it may be beneficial to ask trusted friends and family what they think of your site and ask about what you can improve.

Some things to take a look at include your portfolio section, your "about me" page and your blog (if you have one). Your portfolio on your website should always take center stage, so most of your time should be spent keeping your portfolio up-to-date, well polished, and informative. Add great pieces of work to your portfolio as you complete them and review the existing pieces to see if those that aren't working as well can be removed.

Your "about me" and "services" areas could benefit from a review. Is there something that has changed that should be reflected on these pages? Have you started a new service that isn't in your services listing? Add it so your clients will always have a complete list on what services you offer.

If you have a blog, when was the last time you updated it? I recommend adding a new post to your blog at least once a week. If you haven't been doing this, take a considerable amount of time to write new posts and schedule them so they can be released once per week. Just remember though, you should always be adding to your blog even if you have posts scheduled.

Finally, make sure everything is functioning properly. Is your contact form working? Is your site loading pretty quickly? Are there any broken links? These functionality issues and the overall updating of your site should all be done as soon as possible so that your site is always functioning well and presentable.

Now is the best time to get your website polished. Anything you added to your website to do list is something you can do for this exercise. Spend a considerable amount of time here since your website is your main marketing tool.

7.4 Lecture Social Media, Advertising, Networking and Word-of-Mouth

Being students that live our lives on the World Wide Web, we can use the Internet to help us achieve various types of advertising. However, there are various types of offline forms of advertising as well.

The key to growing your freelance business as a student relies on things you are already good at or are knowledgeable in. As Internet users and consumers alike, we know a thing or two when it comes to using social media and advertising for businesses. However, what other forms of marketing can you use for your freelancing business? Let's cover some of the big forms of marketing you can start using as a student to promote your business.

Social Media

For student freelancers this is probably the number one way we can promote our services. How come? For two reasons mainly: we are already well-versed in various types of social media and we can use it often for free.

Social media such as Facebook, Twitter, LinkedIn and the tons of other social media networks out there are a great place to start spreading the word and promoting your business. Setting up a Facebook page for your freelancing is often the first thing freelancers do and for good reason: you're friends with most of your friends and family on Facebook and they often check it every day. When you promote yourself through Facebook, they will see your services more frequently thus keeping you in mind when they need such services or know someone else who does.

Twitter is another good source of marketing through social media as well. Unlike Facebook, Twitter can help you connect to those you look up to or are well known in your industry. Chatting with them on the regular bases can help you learn but also will open the doors for future opportunities. For example, many of my writing opportunities for large sites came from contacts I made through Twitter.

LinkedIn is another network you can use, however, it is not as often used by students as one would think. It is geared toward professionals which means it is a great way for you to connect with people such as your professors and your current clients. You won't get immediate responses from LinkedIn in terms of getting projects but it can give you credibility when future clients are searching for you or wanting to know more about you.

Advertising

Social media isn't the only type of marketing; you can also advertise as well. Advertising is different from marketing in that advertising is a direct form of promotion. You can advertise yourself through your business cards, sending post cards to prospects, creating and passing out brochures, or taking up ad space on a website or newspaper. These forms of advertising are marketing, but social media, networking, and word-of-mouth are all forms of marketing as well.

Different types of advertising include business cards, post cards, brochures, ad space online, and a website.

I listed several types of advertising above, but the most commonly used with student freelancers are their business cards and postcards. Since you should already have your business card done and printed, let's talk about postcards. A postcard can often provide much more information than a simple business card can. You can create postcards and hand them out with your business cards.

Other types of advertising are worth taking a look at but are often costly. Anything you plan to have printed costs quite a bit to have printed. Other forms such as ad space can start to dig even deeper into your pockets. While some forms of advertising can be beneficial, others can be seen as a waste of your precious dollars. It is worth investigating how well a particular type of advertising is going to help you bring the most return for your money.

Networking

Networking is a more organic form of marketing and is something that can't be done overnight. It is something that takes time to build, however it is often the most fruitful in terms of what will bring you business in the future. There are tons of ways to network so I have dedicated the next exercise entirely to networking.

Word-of-Mouth

A great way to promote your services is by word-of-mouth. Word-of-mouth (WOM) marketing is basically getting people excited enough about your services and what you can do that they tell other people about you. This also can work the opposite way too: if you provide bad services or a bad experience for a client, they will also tell their friends and others about their bad experience and it can hurt you.

Along with networking, word-of-mouth is organic and it takes a while to develop. It is also something you can't directly do on your own. While you can often get your friends and family excited about your services and provide great work to your clients, getting them to share those experiences with others is the hard part. You can ask people to tell others about it, but often it is something others must feel so strongly about your offering they will do it on their own.

One thing to keep in mind about word-of-mouth marketing (something that I hinted to) is to not let bad things about you become WOM. You want only good things to be shared with others. The way to do this is to always consistently provide great service to your clients and strive for client satisfaction. We will talk more about making clients happy in the next lesson.

Other Types of Marketing.

These four types of marketing aren't the only types of marketing that exist. They are, however, the most common and fruitful ones that student freelancers can take advantage of. Something to keep in mind with marketing is anything you do to promote yourself is considered marketing, so be creative! Other forms of marketing includes cold calling, door-to-door visits, promotional materials, and your website!

7.5 Exercise Developing Your Network

For freelancers, networking often makes or breaks their business.

The best clients I have ever gotten were indeed from my network. I didn't even know I was building a network until I started seeing more and more clients come from contacts that I already had. So what exactly is a network and how can you start building yours?

For freelancers, networking is connecting with people and building meaningful relationships with them. These can be vendors such as local printers, other freelancers in related fields as you, or those in an industry you are interested in.

There are several things to remember when it comes to networking. First, think of it like a tomato plant (or any other type of food-producing plant): the more you water it and take care of it, the more it will grow and eventually provide something in return. Networks are something that are built over time and often are not fruitful until after significant time has been put into building one.

Secondly, one shouldn't network strictly in hopes of gaining business. Networking is often a two-way street. When you have people in your network, you should be helping them just as much as you want them to help you.

Finally, networking is organic in nature, meaning that it happens without you directly doing it. That seems a bit counter-intuitive when this exercise is focused on building one, however, you can't simply start networking then stop as if you are moving from one task to another. You're always networking, even when you don't realize it.

Much more can be said about networking and everyone has their own ideas and tips about networking, but for a student freelancer getting started with a small network we currently have can be challenging. In the exercise that follows, we are going to cover a few networking ideas that work best for student freelancers.

DIRECTIONS: In order to start working on your network, you have to get out and talk to people, either in person or online. Below are several networking tips and ideas you can use to build your network. Choose at least three and start working on building contacts with those around you.

1.) Let all your friends, family, and existing contacts know what you do. You have a network of friends, family and others in your life, so why not work it a little bit. Contact them and let them know what you are doing and ask how they are doing. Be creative and find a way to help them with their business or job, be it send them industry-related articles or possibly even prospective clients.

2.) Join local business groups such as the local chamber of commerce and chat with those there. Remember to focus on them, not you. People like when they can talk about themselves so listen to what they say and be ready to ask questions to get to know them. Also, don't forget to get their business card and make sure they get yours!

3.) Join forums online such as freelancing forums or business-related forums. Networking isn't all about your face-to-face meetings. The more you chat with people online, the more they will get to know you. Most of my network contacts that have produced some sort of paying work came from contacts I made online with people I have never even spoke to other than through Twitter or email!

4.) Network with anyone and everyone. Just because you don't think they can directly benefit you doesn't mean they can't in the future. For instance, you would be surprised at how many of your friends may be able to help you in the future if they know someone looking for your services.

5.) Participate in a business expo. Even if you don't have a booth, go to each booth and learn about local businesses in your area. Talk to the representative there and get some information about their business. Chances are they will ask you what you do and that is when you can tell them about your services and hand over a business card.

7.6 Exercise Finding and Getting Your First Client

Often finding your very first project as a student freelancer can be discouraging. So how can you look for and find your first project as a newly minted student freelancer?

Let me be honest; this is the hardest part of freelancing for anyone: finding your first project. Unfortunately, it's a must if you want to start freelancing (besides, how can you call yourself a freelancer if you have no work?). Even after you get your first client, it is a struggle to find new projects and clients all the time. There are a few tricks for a student freelancer just starting out to find their first project, all of which we will cover next.

Non-profit organizations

This one is probably the most common one. Non-profits are typically those who are operating for a different reason than forprofit. Those who are non-profits are charities, churches, private schools (public schools are often funded by the government), and the like. You would be surprised at how many businesses operate as a non-profit.

Look for some of these organizations in your community and see if they need any work done that your skills set can help them with. However, find those you have something in common with. Are you close with your church? Go to them and find out what you can do to help them.

Special Interests and School Organizations

Again, closely related to non-profits, these are groups who often need the help of others to continue spreading their message. Special interest groups in particular are often created for a short period of time, just until the issue is resolved or evolves into something different.

Keep in mind these organizations often don't have a lot of money to pay you for your work (including non-profits mentioned above). You may even be asked to do it for free. This isn't always a bad thing. Yes you have bills to pay, but you also have a portfolio to build and a network to nourish.

Local firms in the same industry

If you are a graphic designer, chances are there are some firms in the area who need help with overflow work. Contacting several of these firms and asking if they hire freelancers for help on projects can help you find projects as well. Although probably not as fruitful as other ways to get projects, this is definitely a good place to start looking.

Job Boards

Another fairly common place student freelancers can utilize to find their first client are job boards. There is a list of such boards in the back of this book. Finding job boards that feature jobs closely related to the type of work you want to do is key. However, the downside to job boards is you often have to work to stand out among tons of other applicants for the same project.

Talking with friends and family

Probably one of the most fruitful ways to find your first project, but maybe not the easiest for some people, is chatting with your friends and family and letting them know what you are doing and what type of projects you are looking for. Ask them if they know of anyone who is looking to hire someone like you. If they give you any names, get in contact with that person right away and talk to them to see how you can help.

DIRECTIONS: Ok, now is the tough part. Going through the different options above, go out there and find your first client! Pick a few of the options above and try them out. Start working at them until you get a project and start work on that project. Once you get a project and you have started working on it, move on to the next lesson!

7.7 Exam What all have you learned about marketing as a student freelancer?

After launching your business comes marketing. How well do you know the marketing aspects of freelancing?

We've covered quite a bit in this lesson with all of the marketing tools you can use to promote your freelancing services. Marketing is such a wide and varied topic that just about any attempts to gain clients could work, but we talked about the big ones that are the most beneficial for student freelancers. How well have you marketed your freelancing business during this lesson? The following exam will help test your knowledge.

DIRECTIONS: Below are a series of statements covering topics discussed in this lesson. Answer each one to see how well you know the ins and outs of marketing as a freelancer.

TRUE   FALSE

T   **F**   1.) Once you get your website up and ready to go, you can let it work for you with no need to keep it updated.

T   **F**   2.) Word-of-mouth marketing is great because it works almost overnight.

T   **F**   3.) Any type of marketing should go through a test period to determine how effective it is for you.

(continued on the next page)

T **F** 4.) Social media is the only type of marketing that works for student freelancers.

T **F** 5.) Two great places to build your network includes joining online forums and participating in business expos.

T **F** 6.) The types of marketing a student freelancer can use successfully depends on their target market.

T **F** 7.) Working with other firms in your industry won't help you find your first client.

T **F** 8.) The bulk of your website—your portfolio—should be the most reviewed part of your site as your skills are constantly changing and the work you produce is getting better.

T **F** 9.) When a student starts freelancing, they should try to market to everyone to drum up clients and projects.

T **F** 10.) Networking requires lots of work up front with making connections with people and is done without hoping for something in return.

SCORING: Check your selections above with the answers below. Each answer has a reference lesson for your help.

1.) **FALSE.** Just because your website is complete doesn't mean you should never look at it again. Your website should be constantly reviewed and updated. *LESSON 7.3*

2.) **FALSE.** Word-of-mouth marketing is something that happens on its own and often takes a while before it becomes fruitful. It's also one of the only things that cannot be directly done by the freelancer themselves. *LESSON 7.4*

3.) **TRUE.** What may work for one student freelancer may not work for others. This is even more so when it comes to marketing. Try out a few types of marketing and monitor how well they work, then stick to the ones that work and phase out the ones that don't. *LESSON 7.1*

4.) **FALSE.** The main types of marketing that tend to work for most student freelancers include social media, word-of-mouth, and networking. Finding a nice combination of these types will serve beneficial to just about any student freelancer. *LESSON 7.4*

5.) **TRUE.** Joining online forums helps you meet people online while business expos help you meet people in person. Both types of networking (online and face-to-face) has its benefits and drawbacks, but a healthy mixture of both can help build your network. *LESSON 7.5*

6.) **TRUE.** If you want to target a specific group, you need to use marketing most likely used by that specific group. For instance, it doesn't make sense to market to college students using AM radio as most college students don't listen to AM radio as much as their iPods. *LESSON 7.2*

7.) **FALSE.** Other firms in your industry are often receptive to hiring freelancers to help when things get busy. Contact them and see if they have any overflow work they may need help on, and produce great work for them. *LESSON 7.6*

8.) **TRUE.** As a student, your skills are rapidly increasing and your portfolio is constantly growing and getting better. You should make sure your online portfolio on your website reflects your best work at any point in time. This means updating it as often as every month. *LESSON 7.3*

9.) **FALSE.** Naturally, most freelancers feel they should try to get everyone to become their client in what is known as "shotgun" marketing. The theory that the more people who know about you the higher chances of landing a client.

However, a freelancer who focuses their marketing efforts on a select few groups of people will actually gain more clients with the same amount of effort. *LESSON 7.1*

10.) **TRUE.** While networking is believed to be the most beneficial for businesses (and is in some cases), the wrong approach to networking is to only focus on those that could bring you business. You don't know who can bring you business, so get to know anyone and everyone. *LESSON 7.5*

GRADE: If you want to put a score on how well you did, below is the formula to help you do just that!

How many you got right: _____ Divided by 10 = _____
x 100 = _____ %

Example: Answered 9 right. 9 / 10 = 9 x 100 = 90%

What's on deck to learn next?

So, what do you do after you gained a client? Everything from communication, professionalism and facing rejection to spotting good and bad clients, dealing with the student factor and working with unhappy clients will be covered in the next lesson. While it seems like working with clients can be a pain, with the next lesson's tips and tricks hopefully you can master working with clients before you ever get your first one!

Lesson 8

Working With Clients

We now know how to gain clients, but how do you work with them? What kinds of things should you expect when you start working with your first freelancing clients? How can you make sure you can deliver what they hired you to do and make sure they are satisfied? What do you do if a client starts treating you differently because they know you are a student?

Not to fear. In this lesson we are going to cover all of the above. Everything from communications skills and professionalism to meeting your first client and spotting good and bad clients are things we will discuss in this lesson. We will also talk about client do's and don'ts, dealing with unhappy clients, and facing rejection.

8.1 Lecture Communication Skills

Have you ever heard the phrase "communication is key?" Ever been in a situation where communication could have helped the situation tremendously?

If you think communicating with others in your every day life can be difficult from time to time, just think about when you are talking to a client and you are nervously sweating and trying to understand their needs.

Probably one of the best tips when it comes to communication is to always strive to be crystal clear. Find different ways to say the same thing. Sometimes it takes repetition to make sure you are not only heard but understood as well.

Appearing and sounding confident goes a long way. Changing your tone of voice to make it seem like you are very confident can make your client feel comfortable and put more trust in you. Sitting up straight, speaking clearly and concisely, and being confident can not only keep you from sounding nervous, but also make you feel more confident and boosts your self-esteem.

Remember there is a lot of non-verbal communication that you need to watch for too. Changes in your client's posture, for one, could signal either interest (if they lean toward

you) or disinterest (if they lean away from you). Eye contact is also something every salesperson and marketing guru will tell you to focus on. Not making eye contact in certain times could signal things such as lack of confidence, lack of knowledge, or even in some cases it could be rude.

When meeting with a client, listen first before speaking and be sure to limit what you to only what is absolutely required, such as asking questions to clarify something they said or to give them additional information.

In summary, watching what you say (verbal) and what you don't say (non-verbal) can all have a great impact on how well you can communicate and how well you are understood. Next time you are talking to your friends or professors, pay more attention to how they communicate, both verbally with what they say and non-verbally with their actions. The more you watch others, the more you tend to pay attention to the things you do. Also, the more you pay attention, the more you adjust yourself, and the more it becomes habit!

8.2 Lecture Professionalism

Now that you are dealing with clients and the public, taking some pointers in professionalism becomes important.

We all feel we act in a professional manner when the times call for it, but for student freelancers we may do things we aren't aware are unprofessional, and these things can turn away clients faster than anything. It's time to take a refresher course on professional behavior when it comes to working with clients and others when it comes to operating a business.

You always want to think before you say or act. As students we are often very laid back, but our clients may not be so laid back. Before jumping in to say or do something, take a moment to think about how your client will react. For instance, using profanity or other harsh language in communications can turn off a client who doesn't use that language. Consideration in the things you say and do should be first and foremost.

Along with watching what you say, in the last section we discussed communication and how what you say and do is being read by your client. These are professional tips as well, as the way you communicate with your client will show your professionalism.

We will talk about it a bit more in the next section, but you should watch how you dress when you go to client meetings too. How you dress depends on the type of client and where you are meeting them, but chances are you probably won't want to wear what you just wore to school to a client meeting after your class. Also, your overall appearance will have an impact on your client too. Make sure you are always well-dressed and well-groomed.

It is important to stress that being professional doesn't mean you have to be perfectly straight-laced and can't joke around. Clients actually like relaxed meetings and don't mind a joke or two. Just keep them clean and appropriate. You can be professional while cracking a joke or two from time to time.

Professionalism isn't just for client meetings either. You should be professional every minute you are on the job. This means responding to client emails in a professional manner, answering phone calls and speaking with clients professionally, and making sure you meet client deadlines on time. You want to act business-like in everything you do, but like I said, it's ok to be laid back as well.

When the results of your marketing plan start bringing you potential business, it's time to think about meeting with your potential clients.

So you got the phone call or email; you have a prospective client who is interested in hiring you to work on their project and they have requested a meeting to discuss more. Oh my! What do you do? How to do dress? What should you bring? What should you say!?!

Slow down and breathe! Freelancers, including student freelancers, meet clients every single day. It is a fact of the freelance world that you will inevitably have to meet with a client to discuss a project.

As with most anything, there are do's and don'ts to meeting with clients. First off, be extremely prepared—even over prepared—for when you meet with them. Often being prepared shows that you are experienced, professional, and it will give you a sense of confidence when you sit down with them.

Keep in mind they are busy professionals. While you are trying to get a clear and detailed picture of their project, you should also be concise and quick with the meeting. Don't be afraid to ask questions, but also be respectful when you start talking and make sure what you say is relevant to what is being discussed. Clients can tell when you are trying to be considerate with their time, and will often give you additional time if needed if you show you are respectful.

Dress appropriately. Every industry has different codes for clothing, but research ahead of time what that industry typically wears. For instance, if you are working with an accountant, then you should probably dress more like a business professional. However, if you are working with a lawn maintenance company, wearing a clean pair of pants and a semi-dressy top will be OK. Under dressing or over dressing is a key to the client that you don't understand them right off the bat and could make them feel highly uncomfortable, so take extra care and plan ahead as to what you should wear.

Arrive fifteen minutes early and don't actually ask the assistant or knock on their door until five minutes before. Often busy clients are working on stuff until the time you are supposed to meet with them. While you want to get there early so you can do last minute prep, you don't want to actually start taking up their time until the time you both agreed to for the meeting.

Also remember that clients should be respectful of your time as well. If a client keeps you waiting with no real reason, chances are they are not being respectful of your time. If your client keeps you waiting, use your judgement about how long you should wait for the meeting.

A general rule of thumb I use when meeting with clients is fifteen minutes. If they are more than fifteen minutes late to the meeting and haven't given me a reasonable reason as to why, that is when I kindly leave a message either on their door (I carry post it notes with me) or with their secretary saying I will follow up with them later.

Facing Rejection.

It's not only student freelancers who are rejected: all freelancers experience rejection from time to time in their freelancing careers. The important thing is to not to get discouraged if your first potential client doesn't work out. There will be times where clients will either turn you down or often just not contact you back at all if they have decided to move on to someone else. If you have been rejected by a client, here are some things to remember: don't get upset or angry, ask for feedback on why you weren't selected, and most of all don't take the rejection to heart as most of the time it has nothing to do with you. Not every client is a perfect match for your services and the sooner you understand this, the easier it is when a client decides to go elsewhere for their project.

8.4 Exercise Creating Your Client Tracking System

There will come a time where you start having to juggle more than one client. How will you manage different clients with different projects at different stages? How about managing prospects and potential projects?

Business is booming and you are starting to become busier and busier. Clients are coming your way and you are starting to work on multiple projects at the same time.

With all of this activity on top of your already busy school schedule, how can you keep your mind straight and make sure you make your clients happy?

In all the freelancing books and articles I've read, I haven't really had any of them come out and say you should have some type of tracking system. Lots of them say you should have some sort of project management system—be it manual or using software—but that often doesn't tell the whole story about what is going on with your business.

What I have figured out works best is what I am calling a client tracking system. I developed a system that allows me to track not only current clients but prospects as well. I like to think of it more as a funnel that funnels into a calendar. Let me expand a bit more.

As you are working on multiple projects with multiple clients, chances are you are also working with prospects who are interested in your services. If I had to take a guess, every single person you are working with are at different stages in the prospect or project time line. It can be crazy to keep track of all of that.

My solution is a funnel-type setup for prospects and a calendar setup for projects. These two combined create a client tracking system. As you can already tell, this is different from a project management system in that I am managing all of the contacts I am working with that could result in money.

In the client tracking system, you can keep track of everything from first contact to final invoice and delivery. That includes tons of steps such as providing an estimate, waiting for approval, waiting for the contract and deposit, and finally starting and moving through the project.

The client tracking system starts with a funnel that ends in a calendar to represent the two types of clients you are dealing with: prospective clients and current clients. Prospective clients move through the funnel while current clients move through the calendar.

In this exercise we are going to set up your client tracking system in a format that is easy to understand and easy to use. The benefits of a client tracking system allows you to see at a glance how your business is going, allows you to follow up with both prospects and current clients, and makes sure you keep every single deadline.

DIRECTIONS: There are two parts of your client tracking system: the funnel and the calendar. Let's work on your prospect funnel then move to your client calendar. We are going to do this in a spreadsheet, but feel free to set it up however you would like.

Prospect Funnel

First, we are going to create a funnel for your prospecting. Your prospecting often varies and requires a lot of info, so we need our system to accommodate this. The info you will need is the client's name/business name, what the current status is, and any specific notes needed (such as where they heard about you from, dates on follow-up, etc.). Remember to keep things like this short and sweet because you want to be able to see at a glance where things stand.

Your funnel should have the following sections in this order: first contact, consultation, estimate/proposal development, estimate/proposal delivery, follow-up, and acceptance. You may find these sections can vary after you figure out what works best for you, but these are good starting sections.

These are pretty self-explanatory: first contact is when a client has expressed interest in a specific project; consultation is when you are finding out the specifics on their project and getting details so you can quote the project; estimate/proposal development is when you are creating the estimate or proposal for your client; estimate/proposal delivery is when you have sent it for review; follow-up is when you discuss with the client your proposal and if they are ready to start; and acceptance is when your client has given you the green light to start work.

The funnel works by putting clients in their respective sections of the funnel depending on what stage of prospecting you are currently at. I do this in a spreadsheet where I have vertical columns that represent each stage, and add the client and their info where they are in the prospecting. My goal is to progressively move clients further down the tunnel toward acceptance.

Create your own system using the mentioned sections in a format that works for you: either using a document on your computer, a spreadsheet, or on paper (although something you can change constantly and cleanly will probably work best). Next, place each prospective client in these sections based on their current status. Make sure to add any information you need to see at a glance to remind you what should be done next.

Client Calendar

Once you have landed a project, you will then add it to your calendar based on your preferred scheduling practices. The reason the client tracking system changes from a funnel to a calendar is because projects are ongoing events that take significant time. To know how much you can take on in the future, you need to be able to see what all you have going on now and in the near future. Using a calendar setup will allow you to see how much you have to do and when you can take on new projects.

Setting up your client calendar is fairly easy: organize projects on the calendar based on their deadlines and how long it takes to complete each milestone. For instance, if it will take me an estimated ten hours to complete a website design and it is due in two weeks, I should allot roughly an hour a day to working on that site design in order to meet that deadline.

You should also add things such as client follow-ups, when to invoice clients, and when clients should be getting back to you with specific items. This should help serve as a daily project list to see what you need to work done and have on every single day at a glance. Be sure to write down specific dates as required.

I use Google Calendar to help me with this, but any type of calendar should be able to help you manage your existing projects. Determine what type of calendar you want to use (paper, Google Calendar, etc.) and put all of your current projects on there based on the information above. Be sure to include things such as what milestone the client is at, what you may be waiting for, and how much you should invoice your client for and when.

8.5 Lecture Spotting the Good, the Bad, and the Ugly Clients

There are good clients and then there are bad clients. Then there are the ugly clients. Let's learn how we can spot each one and how to deal with them.

Not every client you work with is going to be a dream client. You will have the good clients that will always pay on time, bring you great projects to work on, and are just an overall pleasure to work with. You will have bad clients that never seem to pay you on time, always are late getting materials to you, and you cringe when they call you or email you. Unfortunately, you may also get an ugly client too: those who want to tell you how to do your job, who don't respect your work, and overall cause you problems.

With so many different types of clients, how can you spot the good, the bad, and the ugly clients? And after you spot them, how do you deal with them?

The Good Clients

Let's start with the good clients. It is often not hard to spot a good client because they never give you any problems. They always pay you on time and they are very professional in working with you. They respect you and your work and work with you when you ask them for things. Overall, they are the ones that make you love your job.

When you work with good clients, you should go above and beyond for them. They should always be rewarded. If you're working with a good client, go the extra mile and do things like deliver a milestone a few days early, always thank them for when they help make your job easier (by sending things on time, paying you on time), and send them hand-written thank you notes in the mail at the end of the project.

Good clients are the ones you want to nurture and care for the most as they are the ones who are likely to be repeat clients and could benefit your word-of-mouth as well. They are going to appreciate the work you do and will brag about you when they get a chance. Make them happy, and they will be loyal to you.

The Bad Clients

While we all wish we could get good clients, there are some bad clients out there. These are the clients who often pay late, who go M.I.A. for a week or two before contacting you, they want things at the last minute, and/or call at every step of the project.

Bad clients, while they often produce headaches for you, are not entirely hard to work with. Catching on to their ways early will help you respond before things get out of hand. For instance, for clients that insist on paying late make it a point you will stop work on a project until they are paid up. That often gets them moving. Also, if they start taking up a lot of your time with unnecessary or excessive emails or phone calls, explain you will need to charge them for this extra time.

These type of clients are often bad clients because they may not have worked with freelancers before and aren't sure what to expect. Also, they could be like this in their every day life. While they have their own ways of doing business, you need to mold their behavior to work the way you conduct business or you could end up doing a lot more work than you bargained for.

The Ugly Clients

Ugly clients are the ones you should try to avoid, but sometimes the ugly doesn't come until after the project has already started. They are different from the bad clients in that they have many qualities of bad clients or often have the qualities amplified.

Bad clients are those who ask you to do free work after you tell them you don't work for free, they start complaining about your fee and your work even though you know you did a good job, and they want to tell you how to do your job or start questioning how you are working on their project.

The red flags of ugly clients often come out during the prospect phase. Some of these red flags include only wanting a price without giving you any information, not showing trust in your skills and abilities to work on their project, and wanting to withhold information you need. Another large red flag is when they tell you they have worked with another freelancer and "things didn't work out." Not saying who is to blame, but you could be setting yourself up to be the next freelancer who "didn't work out."

Often, I say "don't work with ugly clients," but sometimes you find yourself already knee-deep in a project before you realize the bad client is now an ugly client. The ways you can work with them includes making sure your contract with every client is water-tight and detailed, staying firm and not letting them run over you, sticking closely to the project specs and the contract, and limiting how often they contact you (if they are contacting you every ten minutes).

Assert that you are the professional and they hired you for a reason and take charge of the situation. If worse comes to worse, your contract should state how you can stop work on the project all together. Follow this procedure and "fire" that client. There are far too many good clients out there to suffer through a project with a bad client.

8.6 Quiz Client Do's and Don'ts

Do you know what to do and what not to do when it comes to working with clients? This quiz will test your knowledge and help you learn what to do and not do when it comes to clients.

Most student freelancers haven't worked directly one-on-one with clients until they started freelancing. This can give students the disadvantage of not knowing how to manage client relationships. The following quiz will test your knowledge on what you can do and can't do when it comes to working with your clients on their projects.

DIRECTIONS: Below are several questions about things that student freelancers should and shouldn't do while working with clients. Answer each question based on what you would do to see how well you know how to work with your future clients.

YES   NO

Y **N** 1.) When meeting with clients you should always dress professionally.

Y **N** 2.) It is OK to do free work for clients in order to land their project.

Y **N** 3.) Keep a record of your communications with your client, even if you feel they are an honest client.

Y **N** 4.) You should let your client talk while you listen about their project.

Y **N** 5.) Work to build a relationship with your client before trying to sell to them.

Y **N** 6.) Making yourself appear more experienced and skilled than you really are helps land projects.

Y **N** 7.) If a client says no, you should immediately pack up and go home.

Y **N** 8.) If a client is showing red flags, you should reconsider working with them.

Y **N** 9.) No matter if you have landed the client or the client said "no thank you," stay professional and thank them for their time and consideration.

Y **N** 10.) Always assume the client understands what you say.

SCORING: Think you know all the ins and outs of working with clients? Let's go one by one through each of the questions from the last page to see if you were right.

1.) **DO.** You should always conduct yourself professionally when working with clients including dressing professionally when meeting with them.

2.) **DON'T.** It is a big no-no in the freelance community to do free work—or spec work—in hopes to land a client. Your time and skills are valuable. If a client wants you to do free work, they may not be respecting you or your work as much as you think they are. Always turn down free work unless you want to do free work for organizations such as churches and non-profits.

3.) **DO.** No matter how honest and great the client is, it is professional business behavior to keep detailed records of communications with clients. Often this can be achieved by taking notes for yourself or even as much as reiterating a phone conversation with a client and emailing it to them. Since it is hard to keep track of everything that is said, the best way to remember is to keep a detailed record of it.

4.) **DO.** Let the client talk. You are there to listen about them, their business, and their project. Don't interrupt them and let them give you as much information as they can. Be ready with questions when they are finished talking, but never cut off a client to ask a question. Clients will respect you more if you listen attentively and give them time to talk.

5.) **DO.** Clients hate being sold to. Don't attempt to sell anything, be it you or a service, until you have established some sort of relationship. You can build a relationship by letting them talk first and making sure they feel comfortable with you.

6.) **DON'T.** You should never oversell yourself or make yourself seem better than you are. Doing this sets yourself up to be a disappointment to your client and can only cause problems. If you don't feel confident in your abilities to complete a project, kindly refer the client to someone who can and take time to learn the necessary skills in the future so that you are confident.

7.) **DON'T.** It's OK if the client says no, but that doesn't mean that it's completely over. You can always ask for more information on why they said no. You may be able to learn about something you did and can clarify for the client, or be able to solve their needs in a different way. However, if the client continues to say no, take that as a hint to pack it up and thank the client for their time.

8.) **DO.** You don't have to work with a client who is showing signs of being a problem client. If you are starting to see red flags such as the client being overly clingy or not showing confidence in your abilities, it is completely OK to reconsider working with them and even explain to the client you may not be a good fit. If you are already working on a project with the client, then consider stopping work on the project and "fire" the client respectfully.

9.) **DO.** It is the ultimate sign of respect to always show gratitude toward a client, no matter if they just hired you or decided not to hire you. Always go above and beyond to thank the client for their time and/or for working with you. Remember, karma.

10.) **DON'T.** Clients may not fully understand everything you say when you say it. It is your job to educate the client and make sure they fully understand. Ways to do this include explaining yourself in more than one way, ask the client if they understand what you have said, or ask them if they have any questions you can clarify.

8.7 Lecture Dealing with the Student Factor with Clients

Should you say you are a student, or should you keep it private? What if a client gives you issues for being a student? Let's chat about how to handle the "student factor" of student freelancing.

The student factor. The element that seems to work into a client relationship and may start to cause problems. If you have been freelancing as a student for a bit, you may have run into a client where your student status didn't sit well with them. Either they wanted to get their project done at a lower rate, felt like you weren't as capable as you would be sans-student, or otherwise dislike the fact they are working with an inexperienced professional.

This is a topic that hits close to home with me. Early in my career, I experienced client after client who felt like because I was a student they should get a discount on their project or wanted me to prove myself before they took me seriously. It made me start withholding my student status and started working with clients exclusively online or by phone only.

So, is it better to be up front with a client about your student status, or should you refrain from telling a client that you are a student? After more than five years of being a freelancer, with all but a handful of those months being a student, my suggestion is to not let it come up in discussion, but if it does, be honest. In other words, don't volunteer the information unless you feel it is absolutely needed or the client asks you point blank.

For me, I see it almost like being asked if you are married or not. Your student status has no impact on the project the client is hiring you to do. If you represented yourself accurately and didn't pretend to be someone you aren't, and your school schedule won't impact the normal progression of the project, why should the client care if you are a student?

I've broken this rule a couple of times with good clients (see the previous section about good, bad, and ugly clients). When clients are good and a pleasure to work with, I have told them that I am a student. I haven't had a good client yet have an issue with the fact that I was a student. And why should they if they were receiving the same service they would have if I wasn't?

There are some freelancers, even veteran student freelancers, that may feel differently about keeping the status secret until it is exposed. Some freelancers feel that you should express it up front or when the client wants to get to know you. Others think that you should never ever say it, even if asked. My response to this is that you should always use your best judgement with each client, but never result to dishonesty.

The other side of the coin is if the subject comes up or you are asked point blank if you are a student. You should always be honest with your clients, even if it means it could start causing you problems. Some clients will already know and may never say anything especially if your portfolio is mostly class work or you have said it on your website. Other time clients may get a gut feeling and want to clear it up.

If the subject is brought up or you are asked, it will make you look better and gain the trust of the client if you just come clean. At this point, you should clarify any concerns they have involving your student status such as your experience, skill level, and/or availability.

After the student status has been talked about, clients may feel like they can take advantage of you because you are a student. They may either work to get a lower rate, make you question your experience, or overall give you a hard time because they feel like you don't know what you are doing. Don't let clients bully you because of your student status. Always remain confident and stick to your own policies such as always using a contract, charging the same rates, and never engaging in spec work.

I believe that every student freelancer handles the student status differently. It often takes trial and error to figure out which is the best way to approach the issue. Just remember to always be honest no matter which way you choose to go about the issue.

8.8 Exercise Oh no! Dealing With Unhappy Clients

While you do everything you can to make your clients happy and ensure they are satisfied, sometimes that isn't always the case.

Unhappy clients happen. Every freelancer experiences a client who for some reason or another didn't like how their project turned out or you somehow irritated them. Whatever the reason may be, now you have an unhappy client on your hands and you have to handle the situation.

DIRECTIONS: If you are dealing with an unhappy client, using a combination of the following tips will help calm the situation down and possibly make the client happy again.

1.) Remain calm. There is nothing worse than getting into a screaming match with anyone and it often gets you no where. If you need to, tell the client you will be in touch with them and give yourself some time to think things through and calm down.

2.) Find out the exact reason the client is unhappy. Easier said than done, I know, however if you don't know the real reason, it will be extremely difficult to solve the problem. Keep asking questions and get specific details if at all possible.

3.) If it is your fault, do whatever you can to right the wrong. If you really messed up, own up to it and ask the client how you can correct the problem or present your own solution on how to make things better. We all mess up, but owning up to it and resolving it will often win the respect of your client.

4.) Always remain understanding and apologize if you did something wrong. You want to keep the client calm so showing you understand them and you are taking responsibility for making it right will keep them calm and willing to work with you to resolve the issue.

5.) Refer to the contract if the client is in the wrong. If the client has messed up and it has resulted in problems, kindly and respectfully direct them to the specific clause in the contract related to the issue at hand. Since they signed the contract stating they read and understood it, this should resolve things. If it doesn't and there is no way to make the client happy, it may be time to seek legal representation for mediation.

6.) Your contract is always right. No matter who is in the wrong, your contract is always right. You both signed it, you both have to abide by it. Let your contract be the governing law with any problems. If your contract is water-tight, you should be able to resolve the issue fairly quickly.

7.) If your client is being irate with you, never return the favor. This is rare, but if a client is yelling at you over the phone or being overly irate through email or in person, never start being irate with them in return. You will get yourself in a screaming match and that never solves anything. Calmly calm them down and talk to them. If this doesn't work, then simply tell them that you will work with them after they cool off.

8.9 Lecture Getting Client Testimonials

Potential clients love hearing what other clients think about you and how you've helped them.

Once you finish a project and it is all paid and delivered, the project isn't over. You should look into asking for a testimonial from your client. Testimonials hold a special place when it comes to getting future work. Clients like to hear what others think about you, and what better way to do just that than collect testimonials from your clients.

Asking for testimonials can be very simple but tricky as well. Before you ask for a testimonial, you must first ask yourself a series of questions such as:

- Did the project go as anticipated?
- Is the client happy with the outcome?
- Is the final outcome a portfolio-worthy piece?
- Was the client easy to get along with and would be likely to provide a testimonial?

If you determine a particular client is a great candidate for asking for a testimonial, take a few minutes to craft a well-written email or letter asking them to do so. Be sure to mention you enjoyed working with them and you were glad they contacted you to work on their project. Ask them if they need anything and remind them they can always contact you if they need your help. Afterwards ask if they would be willing to provide a testimonial you can share with others (either on your website, Facebook page, etc.).

Be sure to let them know that providing a testimonial is optional because without providing an out you may receive a testimonial that is not very honest, which would be a waste of everyone's time. I also explain to clients that I use testimonials to help gauge my performance and to see if there is anything I could improve on. I find mentioning that often helps in receiving a very honest testimonial and

additionally any feedback the client may want to give you that could help you in the future.

If a client does provide a testimonial for you, be sure to thank them in more ways than one. Often I reply right away by email then send them a nice hand-written note in the mail the same day so they receive it a couple of days later and will be reminded of the meeting.

Testimonials often help you gauge your performance (didn't I just say that?). When you get a testimonial, you can often determine how satisfied your client is with the project. You could even take the process of getting the testimonial a step further by asking clients what they wish could have been done differently throughout the project.

Once you receive a testimonial, it is important to not change any part of it unnecessarily. If you do change something, you need to make that change in [brackets] so the general public understands something has been changed. I normally shorten my name to just my first name in testimonials to be more personal, so when a client states "Amber Turner did a fantastic job on our website!" I change it to "[Amber] did a fantastic job on our website!" just to keep the testimonial short and sweet and to remain personal and approachable.

Finally, keep in mind testimonials are normally good for a certain length of time. I generally keep all of my testimonials, but publicly display those that have been give to me within the last year. There are certain exceptions to that rule such as if you still do work for the client who wrote the testimonial and that project is still live (for instance you worked on a website for them and they are still sending you work while that website is still live).

Just use your best judgement when using testimonials and when they do expire. If you aren't sure if you can still use a testimonial either because you no longer work with that client or that project is no longer "public" or in use, then it is best just to keep it for your personal files and seek new and updated testimonials from your current clients.

8.10 Exam Are you a whiz at dealing with your freelance clients?

Clients are the heart and soul of your business. Without them, you don't have a business!

This lesson covered many aspects of working with clients, everything from how to talk to clients, meeting your first client, and even to working with difficult and unhappy clients. We also discussed things such as managing the various types of prospects and clients you have and what to do and what not to do when working with clients.

DIRECTIONS: Let's test your knowledge of working with clients with the following questions. Answer "true" or "false" based on the things you learned in this lesson about working with freelance clients.

TRUE   FALSE

T   **F**   1.) You should spill the beans that you are a student when you first start talking to a client about their project.

T   **F**   2.) It is recommended to take considerable amount of time to prepare for every client meeting.

T **F**   3.) Communication is the things that you say and write to clients.

T **F**   4.) Your client tracking system keeps track of your prospects using a funnel and is structured so you can see where each prospect is at a quick glance.

T **F**   5.) If a client is very unhappy and yelling and screaming, you should do the exact same thing back.

T **F**   6.) Professionalism isn't only how you act with others, it also includes what you do when no one's looking.

T **F**   7.) When you have finished a project with a client you feel went great, it's OK to ask for a testimonial and/or feedback about how the project went.

T **F**   8.) When turned down or rejected by a client, there is no point in continuing the discussion or trying to win them over.

T **F**   9.) When meeting with clients for the first time, you should arrive at the scheduled time of the meeting.

T **F**   10.) The difference between bad clients and ugly clients are bad clients may require a bit more of your time but ugly clients are so bad and take up so much of your time you may have to consider firing them.

SCORING: Check your answers above with the correct ones below to find out how well you did. Missed something? Each answer has its corresponding lesson.

1.) **FALSE.** Eh, from my experience it is generally not necessary to tell every client you are a student. Matter of fact, I often don't say anything at all unless it is brought up

or I am asked point blank. Why does it matter if you are a student if you can produce great work and deliver on time? *LESSON 8.7*

2.) **TRUE.** The more prepared you are for your client meeting, the better the meeting will go. You should prepare in every way possible, even if it means being overly prepared. When you take the time to properly prepare, it will show you are professional and it will give you a boost of confidence. *LESSON 8.3*

3.) **FALSE.** Communication includes both verbal action and non-verbal actions. The things you say and/or write has an impact, but it's also the non-verbal communication that plays a key role in the overall communication. Things like eye contact and posture are signals of non-verbal communication that could be saying something different than what you are actually saying. *LESSON 8.1*

4.) **FALSE.** This is only half of your client tracking system. The first part tracks prospects in hopes of making them a client, but it doesn't show you the entire picture of your business. The other part of your client tracking system includes a calendar that allows you to schedule and maintain existing client projects. *LESSON 8.4*

5.) **FALSE.** Never, ever yell or scream at a client, no matter how irate they are. Always remain calm and professional and find out what is really going on. If they don't cool their jets, you should walk away and talk to them at a later time when they are more calm. *LESSON 8.8*

6.) **TRUE.** Most people speak of professionalism in terms of communicating with others, however it is important for the student freelancer to understand professionalism is also in other parts of their business as well. For instance, making sure you meet client deadlines and answer emails and phone calls promptly. *LESSON 8.2*

7.) **TRUE.** Just because you have finished the project doesn't mean you are done. In order to learn and grow as a freelancer you need to find out how you did. This is often done through requesting a client testimonial. You can then use these testimonials in your marketing materials if your client has given you permission to do so. *LESSON 8.9*

8.) **FALSE.** When a client says "no," you should change your strategy and find out why the client said no. Ask them about their decision and see if they are willing to give you more information. If they have concerns, address these concerns. You may not be able to win the client over, but you will walk away with quite a bit of feedback to use for future prospects. *LESSON 8.3*

9.) **FALSE.** There is the idea that if you arrive early, you are on time, and if you arrive on time, you are late. You should arrive to your meeting place at least fifteen minutes ahead of the scheduled time. However, you should only make contact with your client roughly five minutes before because your client often has other things going on up to the scheduled time. *LESSON 8.3*

10.) **TRUE.** Bad clients are not necessarily ones you should kick to the curb. With a little bit of work on your end, it is likely you can turn a bad client into a good client. On the other end, ugly clients often are so difficult to work with and no matter how much time you spend with them, it is unlikely you will be able to benefit from the relationship and should consider "firing" them. *LESSON 8.5*

GRADE: I'm not keeping score, but if you are at home, figure out your score using a little bit of math below.

How many you got right: _____ Divided by 10 = _____ x 100 = _____ %

Example: Answered 8 right. 8 / 10 = .8 x 100 = 80%

What are you going to learn about next?

So far in this book we have covered everything from starting your business to marketing your business, even how to deal with clients. While most of the information shared can go for just about any kind of freelancer, we are a special breed of freelancer: we are student freelancers. In the next lesson, we are going to talk about the big topics where it comes to freelancing as a student such as working during the semester vs. working during the summer, keeping a school/work/life balance, and intermingling school and your freelancing career. I will meet you in the next lesson!

Lesson 9

The Best of Both Worlds: Student and Freelancer

By now your freelance business is moving right along and you are getting to experience all of the trials and tribulations of being a student freelancer. We have been through so much in this book so far from setting up, launching, and marketing your business. Now it is time to talk about a few of the things you will run into as time goes on.

This lesson will cover several aspects of freelancing that can intertwine themselves with your student life. We will talk about working during the semester versus working during the summer, keeping a balance between school and freelancing, the benefits of being a student freelancer, and finally, discuss ways to intermingle your freelancing with your school life and schedule and visa-versa.

Working During the Semester vs. During the Summer

During the school semester, your time is very limited, but once summer rolls around you have increasingly more free time you can use to maintain and grow your freelance career.

When the school semester is in full swing, it starts to become harder and harder to devote time to finding new clients, working on projects, learning new skills, etc. However, often when summer rolls around you start having many more hours in which you can now dedicate to those very important freelancing tasks while still enjoying your break from classes.

Going from Semester to Summer

Taking advantage of the summer months to play catchup and/or get ahead in your freelancing is greatly beneficial for your freelancing career.

There are several things you can do to help boost your freelancing and income during your breaks from school. For starters, you can start ramping up your efforts in marketing, promotion, etc. a couple of weeks before the end of the semester. I know, this may be difficult to do with final exams and projects due at the same time (plan ahead!), but if you can, this is the best time to do it since it often takes about a month to see results from your marketing efforts.

You can start searching freelance boards for gigs and jobs that work with the services you offer to clients. Find the ones that are best suited for you and apply for them. Don't waste your time though sending in applications for jobs that you don't meet 90% of the criteria, because you often won't get a reply back. Check out the resources in the back of this book for a list of various job boards you can browse for freelancing gigs.

One trick that has worked for me and other student freelancers is announce to your present and past clients (more than likely through email) that your schedule is starting to free up some and you are available to take on projects. If your past and present clients have anything you can work on, they could possibly contact you sooner than they originally planned allowing you to start filling up your schedule with work during the summer.

Take time to update your website and marketing materials to reflect any new projects you worked on and any new skills you have learned that would be beneficial to clients looking for the type of services you offer. For instance, if you are a web designer and you now know WordPress, this is not only a great skill to show on your website, but you could add this to your list of services you offer (if you feel comfortable with your new-found skill to be hired for that type of work).

Going from Summer to Semester

So you have a booming freelancing business with all that extra work you did during the summer months, but classes are starting back up again soon. How can you manage to scale back your freelancing to make time for classes?

Several weeks before classes start, work to finish any projects you have outstanding with clients before the first day of class. This helps reduce the amount of work you have as soon as homework starts to pile up.

Take a look and make sure your bookkeeping and record keeping is in order. One of the hardest things to do when your to do list starts to grow is keeping the administrative side of things straight, and unfortunately it is often one of the first things freelancers toss to the side to do later when they have more time. Make sure you have everything in order before school starts so you can avoid potentially forgetting important things such as when you make a purchase or where you stored your tax forms.

Look through your outstanding invoices and follow up on them. Also, invoice for any work you can according to your contract. This allows for income to come in shortly after the first day of classes and allows you time to adjust to less time and less income. Just keep in mind even though money is flowing in doesn't mean you are rolling in the dough. Be sure to put some of it back in your emergency fund or pay any bills due soon.

Start becoming more selective when taking on new work. If a project doesn't seem particularly interesting, doesn't pay well, and/or isn't a good fit for the type of work you do, you may want to go ahead and turn it down so it doesn't take time away from future projects that are in line with the services you offer. The worst thing is having to turn down a really exciting project because you took on a project that wasn't very interesting or rewarding for you.

Finally, don't just stop freelancing all together when classes start back. This isn't good for anyone, particularly your clients who have hired you to perform and for your reputation as you will start to gain the reputation that you will up and leave when you get too busy. Be sure to stay in contact with your clients and return calls right away, just as you would have during the summer.

It is all too easy to start using all of your time to work on freelance projects or learn new things, but the danger lies in not keeping balance with other activities in your life.

Remember earlier in the book when you organized the different activities you have in your life by priority and you stated how many hours you spend for each a week? Are you keeping with that? Chances are you aren't.

When I started freelancing, I started letting it take up more and more of my free time until I was pulling 18-hour days of non-stop work between school and freelancing. I was also working quite a bit on the weekends too. I still find myself working all hours of the day and night just to keep up. Had I planned ahead and took more control earlier, I would not be spending so much time working.

Some things I have implemented in my personal life to keep the school/freelance/life balance seem fairly silly, but they work. For instance, I work on school work after regular business hours. My business hours match everyone else's, and I did that intentionally so it forces me to work on freelance stuff during a certain time. I also make myself go to bed at midnight (unless a disaster happens and I need to work to catch up).

I mentioned not keeping your school/freelance/life balance is dangerous because it starts having long-term effects and they creep up on you without you knowing. Working long hours on the computer, for example, isn't good for your eyes, so taking long breaks from the computer is great for your health. Also sitting in a chair all the time is not good for your back (did you just straighten your posture? I did).

For me, I have always been worried about my health and nothing destroys your health quicker than stress, no sleep, bad eating habits, no exercising, and not staying hydrated. All these things are vitally important to stay on top of. We may be young, but if we don't stay healthy, our bodies will start aging faster.

We also have to keep in mind we are students as well. We can't let our school life slip while trying to maintain a balance with everything else. Our grades should remain high on our priority list, and if they aren't then changes should probably be made so that we can focus back on getting good grades.

Staying Healthy.

I mentioned a little bit that watching your health is important. For all these reasons and more, it is important to stay healthy no matter how busy and hectic your life gets with school and freelancing. Some ways to help stay healthy include setting specific times for exercise activities, cutting back on junk food and eat more healthy food, *drink water instead of sodas, and get at least seven hours of sleep every night. Staying healthy doesn't have to be boring or eat up tons of your time either. Finding clever ways to exercise while doing the other things on your to do list can help like running/jogging instead of walking through your house or apartment.*

9.3 Lecture Benefits of the "Student" Status

Just because you freelance doesn't mean you should suppress the fact that you are a student too. There are several benefits of your student status that can help your freelancing.

I discussed some of the benefits and drawbacks of student freelancing early in this book, but why am I bringing it up again? Well, as you have worked your way through the book, I am sure you are finding ways to put some of those benefits to use. In this lesson I will outline in more detail how to get specific benefits from your student status.

You get all of these awesome benefits being a student, but how can you put them to work for your freelancing business? Once you start to think about it, there are so many ways you can use your student status to help you with various aspects of your business.

For instance, most major software you need to start freelancing offer deep discounts. Take advantage of that! You can start working with professional software at a fraction of the cost other freelancers in the same field have to pay. What a great benefit!

Discounts aren't only limited to software. Once you start looking, you will be amazed at all the places that offer student discounts. If you plan it out just right, you could get most of your first year expenses at greatly discounted prices and be able to save some dough for other things (like your emergency fund).

Another benefit of being a student while freelancing is you have access to many resources on campus. You can ask your professors for advise either in your field or in freelancing which is often not possible after you graduate. There are also resources such as business development centers, resume writing help, and other people on campus who are willing to help you with anything you need.

Don't forget about scholarship opportunities either. There are many scholarships out there looking for students like you who own their own business. You could be right at the top of the line for such scholarships.

These are just a handful of the many ways you can use your student status to benefit your freelancing. Think about all the ways in which being a student is beneficial in terms of discounts, resources and other aspects and see how they can apply to your freelancing.

9.4 Lecture Finding Ways to Intermingle School and Freelance

Finding ways to intermingle your school and freelance life can help you learn and even save you time.

I always like to kill two birds with one stone. Matter of fact, this book is one of them. Late in my college career, I started realizing I could take things I was working on in my freelancing and turn them into school projects, and I could take what I was working on in school and make them personal projects, or use the techniques in my freelancing.

I bring this up because for the longest time I didn't want to intermingle the two, but I soon realized I could save a lot of time and actually learn much more if I meshed the two worlds. Without trying to beat around the bush, what I mean was I was finding ways to use what I was working on in my freelancing as school projects. It worked for my final year as I was able to use several personal projects related to my freelancing as part of my thesis and senior show. This book is one of those projects.

One way you can intermingle the two is for projects that require you to come up with your own idea, see if there are any current freelance projects you could use that would fit those project parameters. If you can, talk to your professor and see if they will let you intermingle the two. That is exactly what I did. When I relaunched my business under a business name, I had a lot of design work I needed to do. I asked my mentor if I could use that for my thesis project and he agreed with no issues.

The bonus is professors will often be glad you are wanting to use something like your freelancing as part of a project in their class. They are often excited to see you take on an additional challenge and because of that, you are more apt to producing higher-quality work.

This can work the other way around too, but is often different. You are in school to learn all you can learn about the field in which you plan to go into. You just chose to freelance instead of seek employment. There are various techniques you are learning right now that you can start using in your freelance practice. Give it a try on one of your next projects. You would be surprised how much you are already intermingling them in your freelance world. I've always said being a freelancer as a student makes you a better student, and visa-versa.

9.5 Exam Know all the ins and outs of freelancing as a student?

Best of both worlds. Didn't think that freelancing as a student had all of those benefits, huh? Let's recap some of the benefits in the following quiz!

Freelancing as a student has its own set of things to deal with on top of being a freelancer. We covered things such as how to transition from freelancing during the summer to the semester and visa-versa, keeping balance in your life, and benefits of the student status.

DIRECTIONS: Circle either "true" or "false" to each of the statements on the next page based on what benefits student freelancers have.

(continued on the next page)

T **F** 1.) Professors often don't like students using outside projects (such as freelance projects) as school projects.

T **F** 2.) Nothing needs to change in your freelance schedule when the fall semester starts back.

T **F** 3.) If you take care of yourself and stay healthy, you can stay productive and never have to fall behind because of being sick.

T **F** 4.) Creativity is key when wanting to intermingle your freelancing with your school work.

T **F** 5.) Since you are living the freelance life, your schedule is very open and fluid to work whenever you want and play whenever you want.

T **F** 6.) Being a freelancer as a student will make you a better student.

T **F** 7.) When freelancing and going to school, you must do whatever it takes to get everything done even if that means letting things like your health and spending time with family should be put on hold.

T **F** 8.) Student freelancers don't get any special benefits over other freelancers when it comes to purchasing software and other things needed for your business.

T **F** 9.) The summer months are a great time for student freelancers to grow their business.

T **F** 10.) There are scholarships student freelancers can apply for that possibly other students can't because they are running their own business.

SCORING: How tough was the exam? Below are the correct answers that you can compare to your answers on the left.

1.) **FALSE.** I am not sure of any professor who would say "no" to students who want to take a school project to the next level by using something in their freelancing as part of the project. However, you should start the conversation with the professor and explain how you want to intermingle a freelance project with a school project if it meets the requirements. *LESSON 9.4*

2.) **FALSE.** When school starts back, most of your free time you had during the summer will be dedicated to classes and homework. You won't have as much time to work on projects. Take a few weeks before the start of the semester to wrap up projects as much as possible. *LESSON 9.1*

3.) **TRUE.** Exercise, eat right, get plenty of rest, and overall take care of yourself. When you run yourself ragged you increase your chances of getting sick, which means you increase your chances of having to take unexpected time off to get better. With your schedule being so busy, you can't afford down time like this. *LESSON 9.2*

4.) **TRUE.** Not every school project will lend itself nicely to a freelance project and visa-versa. It took me several years before I was able to figure out how to make a freelance project a school project, but once I did it saved me lots of time, I learned much more than I thought I would, and often made higher grades. *LESSON 9.4*

5.) **FALSE.** While it is true being a freelancer does have its flexibility benefits when it comes to your schedule, it also means you must work even harder to keep your life in balance. You should determine the important things in your life and keep them in balance even when your schedule is slam full. *LESSON 9.2*

6.) **TRUE.** Being a student freelancer makes you pay more attention to your class projects and things you are learning in school because you know how important these things are based on your experiences freelancing. You take projects more seriously, you strive to produce better work, and overall take a greater interest in your coursework than you probably would have otherwise. *LESSON 9.4*

7.) **FALSE.** While you are really busy now and may not have time for everything, you should still make the important things in your life a priority such as your health and your family. Often this means giving up on some activities such as watching TV or playing games to make sure you stay on top of your priorities. *LESSON 9.2*

8.) **FALSE.** Who said you can't use your student status to get some great discounts on things for your business? For instance, most student freelancers need expensive software that can be purchased at a discount if you show proof of being a student. Why not take advantage of this? *LESSON 9.3*

9.) **TRUE.** You now have so much more free time than you did before, some of which you can dedicate to new client projects. Increase your marketing efforts during your off months to take advantage of this extra time you have. *LESSON 9.1*

10.) **TRUE.** There has been an increase in scholarships that are made specifically for those students who own their own business or who have the entrepreneurial spirit. Being a student freelancer immediately makes these scholarships a great opportunity for you to help pay for school. *LESSON 9.3*

GRADE: This is one grade that only you will know. Use the formula below to see how well you did.

How many you got right: _____ Divided by 10 = _____
x 100 = _____ %

Example: Answered 7 right. 7 / 10 = .7 x 100 = 70%

What are we going to cover in the lass lesson of this book?
Well, now that everything is moving along in your freelancing business as a student, we will be covering some aspects of your freelancing that will help take it up a notch. Learn when to raise your rates, what to do when you become too busy, staying organized, specializing in a specific niche, and working on side projects. Let's wrap up this book with the final lesson!

Lesson 10

The Next Steps In Your Freelancing Career

While most of this book has been dedicated to the beginning of your freelancing career, and the last lesson was dedicated to your student status, in this final lesson we are going to cover aspects of your student freelancing that will help take your freelancing to the next level. Once business is booming and things are clicking, you may want to start evaluating things and making room for new and exciting changes.

In this final lesson, we will talk about aspects of freelancing most freelancers encounter in their careers. Since we are student freelancers, we may run into some of these even before we graduate. We will talk about everything from evaluating your success to setting goals, staying organized to getting additional help when needed, even when to raise your rates to starting a side project!

10.1 Exercise Evaluating Your Success

You've come a long way from thinking about freelancing as a student to actually freelancing as a student, so how well are you doing now?

Clients are contacting you, projects are rolling in, you are starting to make good money and business is good, or is it? Once you have gotten the hang of your freelancing, it is always good to take a step back and evaluate not only yourself but your business as well. Do you feel that you are a successful freelancer?

There are several things to consider when evaluating yourself and your business. Let's start with evaluating yourself. How much have you learned since you started freelancing? Are your skills improving and/or expanding? Have you made changes in your life to allow for you to take on this new freelancing world? These are just a handful of questions to think about when evaluating yourself.

When it comes to evaluating your freelancing business, however, there are many more things to consider. Did you meet your goals? Are you making money? Is your client list consistently growing? These questions and many more are those we are going to cover in this exercise.

DIRECTIONS: Self-evaluation is never easy, but as a self-employed student freelancer you are the only one who can evaluate the success of your decision to start freelancing. Below are some questions to consider about your time as a student freelancer. Go through them and write down your thoughts and answers. You are the only one that will read these responses so be honest with yourself.

Evaluating Yourself

How have you personally grown since starting your business? Are you more organized than you were before? Do you feel more responsible since you started freelancing?

_____

_____

_____

_____

How has your life changed since becoming a freelancer? Are you more or less busy than you were before?

_____
_____
_____
_____

How are your academics going? Have you noticed a change in your grades (for better or worse)? Are you still able to commit enough time to your homework and studies?

_____
_____
_____
_____

How is your skill level? Do you feel you have learned more since you starting freelancing? How about your business skills?

_____
_____
_____
_____

Evaluating Your Freelance Business

Did you meet any of your goals you set out earlier in this book? What goals have you met and which goals have you not met yet? Have you made new goals?

_____
_____
_____
_____

(continued on the next page)

Are your clients happy with the work you are producing for them? Do you find it easy to work with clients or are clients difficult to work with?

_____
_____
_____
_____

How is your income? Are you making your hourly rate on projects? How is your expenses in relation to your income?

_____
_____
_____
_____

Are you more satisfied with you career choice since becoming a freelancer? Has freelancing and your business changed your outlook on your career or your future plans?

_____
_____
_____
_____

Right now, do you feel your business is successful? What about your business is successful? What parts of your business could use some improvement?

_____
_____
_____
_____

Staying Organized Through the Fast & Slow Times

One of the first things to start slipping when things get busy is organization of files and folders, be it on paper or on your computer.

I will be the first to tell you when projects, assignments, tests, exams, etc. start piling up, it can be easy to forget to take care of certain things. Often what happens is you become less organized because you are limited on time.

It is always worth staying organized no matter if times are fast and your to do list is long or if times are slow. Seems like a no-brainer, but when things start to get busy, you may start forgetting certain details about projects you are working on or if you have any outstanding invoices that need to be paid. If you aren't organized, it may eat up even more time to find out about these things.

However, if you stay organized and create systems to keep track of things like invoices, payments, client phone calls, client requests, estimate requests, emails, etc., when things become hectic, staying organized is second nature.

It helps to take the couple of weeks before school starts, major breaks you get during the semester (fall break, winter break, spring break), and when you get out of school for the year to get all of your ducks back in a row. Spending a few hours to get reorganized and on top of things not only makes it easier down the road, but it reduces what is on your to do list, it will save you time later when you need

If you organize yourself right from the start, managing that organization takes next to no time when you are busy.

to find information quickly, it reduces your stress (which will help your health), and it won't be so difficult later to get reorganized if something happens.

There is no right or wrong way to staying organized. It is OK to develop your own systems where it comes to keeping track of invoices, email, etc. For instance, I keep track of all of my freelancing financial stuff (income, expenses, payments, invoices, projects, etc.) in a Google Docs spreadsheet and I share it with all of my email accounts. That way no matter which email I am logged into, I can always access it.

10.3 Lecture Specializing and Finding a Niche

When you began your freelancing career, chances are you were a jack-of-all-trades freelancer. When is the right time to specialize your services and/or find a niche?

Jack-of-all-trades freelancers are those who do a large range of services. Pretty much anything the client needs they can deliver. However, most freelancers feel they can earn more in their freelancing if they specialize in a specific area of their field.

For instance, web designers and developers often want to specialize in one particular area such as around a content management system like WordPress or around a particular area such as search engine optimization. While they can do other things such as print design and develop websites, they often stick to one type of work and specialize in it to become an expert in that speciality.

Specializing in a specific area of freelancing has its benefits and drawbacks. Some benefits of specializing in freelancing include becoming an expert in that specialty, demanding higher rates for their services, and often carve their own niche in the marketplaces.

However specialization has its drawbacks too, such as becoming obsolete when the service is no longer desired, quickly becoming bored of doing the same thing over and over, and possibly maxing out your potential income earnings by not differentiating your services.

As a student freelancer, the idea of specializing often comes after a couple of years of freelancing when you start figuring out you are excelling in a specific area or clients are hiring you to perform a specific service.

Student freelancers will find it easier to specialize in a specific area when they notice their portfolio is becoming more focused and they are more knowledgeable in a particular area. However, for student freelancers starting out, they may find it more difficult to specialize because they know a little about a lot of things, but not a lot about certain things.

Specializing in one area isn't an overnight decision and often doesn't result in overnight success. It requires a major shift or change in the way you conduct business and it could impact your income negatively in the short run.

If you are considering specializing in a specific area, do your research and evaluation on your own business and your own skills. Keep in mind, however, it requires much work in making the specialty work in your favor and often is fruitful after several months of focused effort.

10.4 Lecture When Should You Start Increasing Your Fees?

Been freelancing for a bit and wondering if it is time to raise your rates? Chances are you are right.

Student freelancers are in a unique situation where our skills and knowledge are growing much faster than most other freelancers. With your growing experience and skills increasing, chances are your rate you started out with probably needs a revision.

When your experience is increasing and your skills are improving, you are growing as a freelancer and you are now able to provide even more knowledge and solutions for your clients. You should start being compensated more for this increase in knowledge.

The rule of thumb is you should raise your rates once a year to stay on par with the cost of living and your experience. Since your experience and skill level should never decline, it is safe to say they will always go up every year. This is even more true for student freelancers, and this rate increases even faster while you are in school and will slow down after you graduate.

If you have been freelancing for a year, you should consider increasing your rate a bit. Why? You probably underpriced yourself from the start because you were just starting and didn't feel you could command a higher rate. Now you feel more confident and can afford to charge higher rates. For me, I raised my rates $10 per hour every year until my last year of college. Now that I have graduated, my rate may not go up as high every year.

The worry with raising your rates is you may not gain as many clients as you were before. This is true in some cases for clients who are looking for your rate level, but also false in that when you raise your rates you are moving into a different rate level and open yourself up to more clients on the higher end of the budget range who are willing to pay higher rates. These higher rates will balance out having fewer clients.

You can raise your rates one of two ways: raise it across the board for new and existing clients all at once, or raise your rates for new clients and raise your rates only for new projects with existing clients.

If you are raising rates on existing clients, do your clients a favor and give them a heads up that your rates are going up and to talk to you if there is any concern. If they are good clients they more than likely will not flinch at your rate increase.

Raising your rates also gives you the opportunity to find more and better clients. Like I said before, you are now opening yourself to higher budget clients who may not have considered you before because your lower rates. You will start noticing you don't have to take on difficult or problematic clients or projects when your rates are a bit higher because new clients will fill those spots.

10.5 Exercise **Setting Goals for the Future**

Love 'em or hate 'em, setting goals and working to achieve them keeps you motivated and focused. Without goals, we can never focus our energies to grow our business.

Now that you are well on your way to becoming the next big freelancer (or at least support yourself when you graduate), you should start thinking about what you want to achieve with your new freelancing business. Instead of just hoping and wishing to achieve certain things, creating goals that are aligned with those wishes helps provide a motivator for you to reach for those goals.

Before we get into goal setting, there is a certain way in which you should think about goals when creating them. I am sure you have heard it before, but for completeness, let's talk about SMART goals.

SMART goals stand for "Specific, Measurable, Attainable, Realistic, and Timely." Although fairly self-explainable, let's hit each one briefly.

Specific means answering a series of questions about the goal such as asking "Who, What, Where, When, and Why" questions to make sure your goal is very detailed and to-the-point. If you can't answer all of these questions, the goal is not specific enough and you need to refine it.

A goal is measurable when there is some way for you to measure if you are getting close or not. One way is to break down your goal into mini goals or tasks and mark them off as you get there. Another way is to put time limits for parts of the goal in order to reach the bigger goal in time.

A good indicator on if your goal is measurable or not is if it involves numbers (meaning it is quantitative). For example, if you are trying to lose (or gain) weight, you wouldn't set a goal for "losing weight until I look the way I want" because that goal has no end. However, a goal that is measurable would be "lose 10 pounds." This allows you to objectively know if you are getting close or have met your goal.

Attainable and realistic are fairly close to each other, but they mean you must be able to achieve them, and they are realistic in the manner in which you plan to achieve them. Goals could be attainable, but not realistic. Basically the difference between the two is that attainable means that anyone could do it, where as realistic means that you can do it.

Timely is the final part of SMART goal setting. You must put a time table on your goal. Remember the first aspect—be specific in that timing. For instance, state you plan to achieve your goal by the start of the semester or plan to finish off a project by the new year. This also ties into being measurable. If your goal is to do something by a specific date, write that date down or circle it on your calendar.

Now that we know what SMART goals are, we are going to work through setting short-term and long-term goals. The definition for short-term and long-term goals very, but for the purpose of this exercise, short-term is anything in the next two years, and long-term is more than two years. After all, we are still students and in two years we could be graduating and have different career plans.

DIRECTIONS: Keeping the SMART goals concept in mind, let's work through making at least three short-term goals and three long-term goals relating to your freelancing you can work toward. Don't limit yourself to three for each though; if you have more then feel free to jot those down as well. Also, remember to keep your dreams and wishes in mind, and work to make sure these goals are aligned to your wishes.

Short-Term Goals

Remember short-term goals are ones that are within the next two years (at least for students). With that in mind, what are some things you want to achieve before you graduate? Would you like to hit a specific income goal? A certain number of clients? Think about what you want to achieve and write down the goals below. Make sure they hit every aspect of SMART goals so they are rock solid. I've given you some lines to help you keep them organized.

1.) _____

_____

2.) _____

_____

3.) _____

_____

Long-Term Goals

Let's repeat the same process for long-term goals, or goals further than two years away. Another way to think about it is goals you want to achieve close to or after graduation. Want to start hiring employees? What about getting your own office space? Write out in detail your long-term goals below so that you can stay focused. It also wouldn't hurt to write out mini-goals to help you accomplish these long-term goals. Below are some lines again to help you keep track of your long-term goals.

1.) _____

_____

2.) _____

_____

3.) _____

_____

10.6 Lecture Can't Handle the Load? When to Start Collaborating

You've worked so hard to develop your freelancing, and you are starting to have clients regularly hiring you for projects. Things are moving along just the way you had hoped it would, but now it's moving along too much.

Freelancers tend to have slow times and busy times. For a student freelancer, however, this tends to happen at the worst times. You are either slow during the summer or very busy during final exams. It is great to be busy and working on projects all the time as a student freelancer, but maybe you have gotten to the point where you can no longer keep up with your current project load.

What is a student freelancer to do when this happens? There is only so many hours in a day for student freelancers to do everything from homework to classes, chores to their freelancing. How is a student freelancer supposed to be able to make their clients happy and keep their grades up?

The one thing to keep in mind as freelance projects start piling up is focusing on what you do best. If you see yourself starting to take on projects that are not in your list of services, stop taking on that kind of work! Find other (student) freelancers who do that type of work and send it to them. Are you a web designer? Then don't take on projects for logo design—find another freelance designer who does logo design well and send them the project. Besides, you never know when that freelancer may return the favor (trust me, they will return the favor)!

> *One way to help reduce your work load is to hire other freelancers who can help with your overflow work.*

The best solution, and one many freelancers do from time to time, is collaborate with other freelancers on projects to get the job done. Are you better at designing websites than coding them? Find a web developer freelancer who could help you out on a project. Do you enjoy taking photographs more than retouching them? Find a freelance retoucher who can do the work better and faster than you can.

You can also find other freelancers just like you who may need some work. If you have too many projects going, send one to another freelancer who is searching for work. Helping other freelancers out not only makes you feel good but they will remember it and keep you in mind for when they may need to do the same thing.

Often when freelancers do this, they manage the project themselves, working directly with the freelancer on behalf of the client. It is not uncommon for a freelancer to estimate a project for a client by taking the estimate from another freelancer who will be doing the work and adding a percentage to manage the project so they can earn some money as well without doing all the work. As long as the other freelancer knows about this, it is a good way to make a bit of extra money without having to do a lot of extra work.

One small note to keep in mind: be careful when you start outsourcing work. Be especially particular about sending clients to other freelancers. Make sure these other freelancers are trustworthy and produce quality work. The work they produce for the client says just as much about the freelancer as it does about you.

10 Successful Habits of Student Freelancers

Student freelancers are successful for many different reasons. Do you have some of these habits of successful student freelancers?

Student freelancers succeed when they establish habits that work for them. Everyone has their own recipe for success, however, there are some common habits all student freelancers have. In this quiz, there are ten habits that are common among student freelancers. Take the quiz to see if you have some of these habits!

DIRECTIONS: Below are ten habits of successful freelancers. Answer "yes" or "no" to the following statements based on if you have these qualities.

YES   NO

Y **N** 1.) You don't undervalue your work and you charge what you feel you are worth.

Y **N** 2.) You always start every project with a signed contract and a deposit in hand.

Y **N** 3.) You are able to balance many different things, from school to client projects to your personal life.

Y **N** 4.) You find ways to "wow" your client such as going the extra mile and always thanking them for their time.

Y **N** 5.) You market yourself even when your project schedule is full.

Y **N** 6.) You've developed a system to handle everything about your business, from prospects to clients, contracts to projects, and invoices to payments.

Y **N** 7.) You deliver consistent results and ensure client satisfaction with follow-ups after projects are complete.

(continued on the next page)

Y **N** 8.) You never let rejection take you down and you use rejection as a way to become a better freelancer.

Y **N** 9.) You spend time on developing your skills and knowledge outside of school work and client work.

Y **N** 10.) You genuinely love what you do and enjoy what you do every day.

SCORING: If you answered "yes" to all of the above, you have the habits of a successful student freelancer! Did you answer "no" to something above? Now is a great time to make that your new habit!

10.8 Lecture Should You Continue Freelancing or Find A Full-Time Job?

You've been freelancing for a while, and graduation is right around the corner (or you just recently walked across the big stage). What should your next move be?

For many student freelancers, when graduation is right around the corner or a recent memory, their freelancing career starts to get heavily scrutinized as mounting pressure to make a full-time income becomes more and more pressing. It's natural for a student freelancer to be questioning their freelancing when it seems easier to go seek full-time and steady employment.

Since this is a natural thing for most student freelancers to experience, it is worth discussing some things to consider when you start having this discussion with yourself.

The number one factor in deciding if you should continue to freelance or seek full-time employment is money. We all have different monetary needs and when we graduate (or come close to it) these monetary needs change drastically.

Also, every student's situation is different and likely to change upon graduation.

With money being the major driving factor for student freelancers when considering full-time employment, it is no surprise many student freelancers do seek steady employment within the first year of graduation. This is the case either because they suddenly find themselves needing to fully support themselves, their student loans quickly become due and lack of funds to cover it is causing stress, or because they are getting pressured by family to seek a job instead of working from home.

Whatever the case may be, as a student freelancer you have to decide if you should continue freelancing, if seeking full-time employment is the best option, or a combination of both. Some things to consider includes your available time, what you are making now as a freelancer, your personal monetary needs, and any outside forces that may be pressuring and influencing you.

While money is a main motivator when it comes to choosing between freelancing and steady employment, student freelancers often consider other things as well. For some, the massive amount of available time after school and classes are history allows for some freelancers to market themselves even more to keep their freelancing careers.

Others see it as an opportunity for change and want to seek employment.

How your freelancing success is currently is another factor. For student freelancers who see their freelancing as successful and growing, they will stick with freelancing after graduation. However, for those who don't feel freelancing is for them, they will quickly stop and look for other forms of employment.

Finally, outside forces such as parental pressure and mounting bills are often factors for freelancers who aren't making enough to satisfy either their parents or their bills (or both). Employment is a way to start making a full-time income and be able to satisfy many external pressures.

If you do decide freelancing is for you, then graduation provides many benefits such as an increase in the time you can spend on your business and a reduced stress level. It also provides you a means to personally develop yourself through client projects and allows you to work on what you want to work on.

However, if moving to a full-time job is the best option for you, making the transition has its benefits and drawbacks. First, you have to figure out how to deal with your current clients: are you going to finish their projects or refer them to another freelancer? You can't up and leave your clients hanging and not knowing what happened to you.

A drawback to going job hunting is some employers may not feel your freelancing experience in college is the equivalent to having your own business or "job experience." You may have to prove yourself even more to obtain a job because of the idea that freelancing isn't really a job (even though you and I both know differently).

Whatever your decision is, make sure it is the right one for you right now in your current situation. Your goals and desires should help guide you in the right direction, where your current needs such as money and external forces may play into a pretty big decision right after the big show and getting that hard-earned diploma.

10.9 Lecture Starting and Working on Personal Side Projects

I personally love side projects! Matter of fact, this book was one of those side projects!

I don't know any freelancer who don't have something outside of their freelancing they love to work on. Why is that? For many reasons (most of which I will outline below), it helps keep you motivated and on top of your game.

So what do I mean by side projects? These are often projects you want to work on that aren't necessarily for a specific client, but are closely related to your freelancing. For example, some of my side projects include *Students That Freelance* obviously, this book was one of those side projects, and my personal website amberturner.com that

I like to use as a testing ground for really neat technology and allows me to stretch my creative muscle. Since I am a graphic and web designer and self-employed, all of these projects are closely related to my freelancing and helps me develop as a freelancer.

Side projects can be anything from working on another business model (if you are a web developer you could start working on a specific software that would help other web developers), write about your experiences or new things in a blog (like I do with *Students That Freelance*), or anything!

Like I stated earlier, there are tons of benefits for starting and working on side projects in addition to your freelancing. Probably the most important reason (and the reason I talk about it in this book) is it helps you develop more as a creative professional in your field. Another closely related reason is it can help you establish yourself even more as an expert in your field.

Who says these side projects can't be related to your schooling? I am all for finding ways to intermingle school and freelancing when you can. Maybe the school department in your field of study needs a new website? One example I seen in the business department at my school was there were several seniors that started a resume site for graduates and alumni. They developed a way to collect resumes and send them out to local business owners and companies seeking to hire recent grads. They took their business skills and created a very helpful service for other students.

Another benefit of side projects is they could potentially become an additional source of income. When I started this book as a joint school project and side personal project, I didn't think about publishing it until started on it. I soon realized I just opened up a great potential for additional income by publishing and selling this book. A side project with a possibility of a little green in my pocket? Yes please!

10.10 Exam Ready to take your freelancing up a notch?

Taking the next steps in your freelancing career can be exciting and nerve-racking all at the same time.

We've been through a lot throughout this book together, and now you have a thriving freelance business to show for it. And can you believe you are still just a student? Feels amazing to know you have started your career and you are your own boss. Your business is growing and you are looking for ways to take your freelancing to the next level.

In the last lesson of this book, we talked about the next steps in your freelancing career including evaluating your success, staying organized, specialization, if and when to raise your rates, collaboration, successful habits, and side projects. Let's test your knowledge on how you can take the next steps in your student freelancing career.

DIRECTIONS: Below are ten questions about topics found in this lesson. Answer each one by circling "true" or "false" for each statement. Afterwards, review your answers to see how much you learned in this lesson.

TRUE   FALSE

T   **F**   1.) When evaluating your success as a student freelancer, you should evaluate only how your business is growing, leaving personal growth out of the success equation.

T   **F**   2.) For most freelancers, including student freelancers, raising your rates should be considered at least once every year.

T   **F**   3.) Graduation raises many questions for a student freelancer, including deciding if continuing their freelancing is right for them or if they should seek steady employment.

T   **F**   4.) One habit of successful student freelancers includes starting projects with only a deposit in hand.

T   **F**   5.) It is recommended for student freelancers to take the final few weeks of summer vacation to wrap up freelancing projects so the start of the new semester won't be so hectic.

T   **F**   6.) Specializing in one type of freelancing is great for the student freelancer who gets bored easily doing the same thing over and over again.

T   **F**   7.) Setting goals is only something a student freelancer should do before they start freelancing.

T   **F**   8.) One of the several benefits of personal side projects for student freelancers include the possibility of additional income.

T **F** 9.) When you get too busy to handle your current freelance load, an option to help ease the load is collaborating with other freelancers (possibly student freelancers) to help you get projects done on time.

T **F** 10.) Having systems in place before you get busy can help you stay on top of things when your schedule and to do list starts filling up.

SCORING: Check your answers against the explanations below to see if you were right. If you missed one, review the explanation and the section it relates to if necessary.

1.) **FALSE.** As student freelancers, we are constantly growing both personally and professionally. While it is important to evaluate our business success in terms of income and clients, the other half of our success should be determined on personal factors such as experience and skill level changes. *LESSON 10.1*

2.) **TRUE.** Most freelancers raise their rates once a year because of increases in cost of living and their experience. The only difference with student freelancers is most student freelancers' experiences and skill levels increase more rapidly while they are in school compared to freelancers who are not enrolled in school. *LESSON 10.4*

3.) **TRUE.** Your life changes after graduation, which means you may have to make change to your freelancing career as well. For most student freelancers, the decision is either to continue freelancing or seek full-time employment. This decision is often influenced by factors such as external pressures and monetary needs. However, it is becoming increasingly popular among student freelancers to still continue freelancing while seeking full-time employment. *LESSON 10.8*

4.) **FALSE.** While a deposit is a good thing to have before you start a project, you should also take the precautionary measure of having your client sign a contract. Not only is it professional behavior to have in writing what you will be doing for the client, you shouldn't start any work without having everything clarified and agreed upon for the client. *LESSON 10.7*

5.) **TRUE.** Part of staying organized no matter how busy you are is preparing for major changes in your schedule, such as the start of a new semester. We discussed one way to prepare yourself for the new semester is to wrap up current projects to reduce your stress level. *LESSON 10.2*

6.) **FALSE.** Quite the opposite tends to be true. Freelancers who like to have a mix of projects to work on and dislike working on the same thing day in and day out should not consider specializing unless there is some other major benefit to doing so. Student freelancers who specialize can find themselves working on the same kind of project for various clients. *LESSON 10.3*

7.) **FALSE.** No matter where you are in your freelancing career—be it at the very beginning or a few years in—making goals and working toward achieving those goals is important. In this lesson we discussed making goals after starting your freelance business, but earlier in the book we also made sure to set goals before we even took on the first client. *LESSON 10.5*

8.) **TRUE.** Depending on the type of side project you start, you could potentially find a way to make money with it. Be it either making saleable graphics, making stock imagery, or even writing a book; many different types of side projects for freelancers result in additional income. *LESSON 10.9*

9.) **TRUE.** Student freelancers are already extremely busy, so taking on a few client projects could prove more than they can handle. We discussed how to help with this by collaborating and hiring other freelancers to work on parts of the project you may not want to do or don't know how

to do as well. This is also a common occurrence with other freelancers. *LESSON 10.6*

10.) **TRUE.** Having systems in place to manage things such as clients, projects, invoices, and income before you start getting busy can help save you time when you start filling your calendar with client projects. The key thing to remember, however, is to keep these systems simple so that it doesn't take up any unnecessary time to manage it. *LESSON 10.2*

GRADE: Did you nail all of them correctly, or did you miss a few? Below is the formula to calculate your grade, if you keep track of these kinds of things.

How many you got right: _____ Divided by 10 = _____ x 100 = _____ %

Example: Answered 9 right. 9 / 10 = .9 x 100 = 90%

Special Goodies

Extras

Conclusion Wishing You Well Wishes!

It has been quite a journey through this book! If you have made it to this section, I must congratulate you on your new freelancing career and thank you for hanging in there with me throughout the book!

I hope this book has helped you gain the confidence, knowledge, motivation, and determination to not let anything stand in your way of what you would like to accomplish as a freelancer while you are in school. Student freelancers are a rare breed and I admire you for not only picking up a book like this, but going through it and sticking to your goal of becoming self-employed!

It was my intent for this book to serve as a one-of-a-kind resource for student freelancers, so I hope I did not disappoint! Now that you have made it all the way through, don't forget you can always go back and reference any topic in this book should you feel you need help in certain areas. Any book on freelancing (including this one) is not meant to be a "one time read" but to be a constant resource for any issue you come across, and I hope this one can serve as your go-to resource!

With deepest sincerity, I wish you all the best in the world with your future freelancing business, and most importantly I want to congratulate you on your future graduation as well! It takes a lot of determination and hard work to not only finish your education and walk across that stage, but doing so while starting and running your own business! I wish you much success, and I hope to hear of your future successes!

Best Wishes!!

– Amber

Resources

There is tons of information online and in books that can help you develop your freelancing career even more. Check out these resources to find more information on just about any topic you need help with.

Websites

- Freelance Advisor (UK): freelanceadvisor.co.uk
- FreelanceFolder: freelancefolder.com
- FreelanceShack: freelanceshack.com
- FreelanceSwitch—Freelance Jobs, Forum and Directory: freelanceswitch.com
- Guerrilla Freelancing: guerrillafreelancing.com
- Life of the Freelancer: lifeofthefreelancer.com
- Student's Guide to Web Design: studentguidewebdesign.com
- ULancer: ulancer.com

Forums

- FreelanceFolder Forums: freelancefolder.com/forums
- FreelanceSwitch Forums: forum.freelanceswitch.com

Job Boards

- 37 Signals Job Board: jobs.37signals.com/jobs
- Authentic Jobs: authenticjobs.com
- FreelanceSwitch Job Board: jobs.freelanceswitch.com
- Jobpile: artypapers.com/jobpile
- Krop: krop.com
- Search Web Jobs: searchwebjobs.com
- Smashing Jobs: jobs.smashingmagazine.com

Books and Guides

- "100 Habits of Successful Freelance Designers" by Steve Gordon Jr. and Laurel Saville. ISBN: 9781592535125
- "The Business Side of Creativity" by Cameron S. Foote. ISBN: 9780393732078
- "Career Renegade" by Jonathan Fields. ISBN: 9780767927413
- "Creative, Inc." by Meg Mateo Ilasco and Joy Daengdeelert Cho. ISBN: 9780811871617
- "Creatively Self-Employed" by Kristen Fischer. ISBN: 9780595421547
- "Escape from Cubicle Nation" by Pamela Slim. ISBN: 9780425232842
- "Freelance Confidential" by Amanda Hackwith. ISBN: 9780987102607

- "Freelance Design in Practice" by Cathy Fishel. ISBN: 9781600613029
- "Graphic Artist Guild: Handbook for Pricing and Ethical Guidelines" 12th edition. ISBN: 9780932102133
- "A Graphic Design Student's Guide to Freelance: Practice Makes Perfect" by Ben Hannan. ISBN: 9731118341964
- "The Money Book" by Joseph D'Agnese and Denise Kiernan. ISBN: 9780307453662
- "My So-Called Freelance Life" by Michelle Goodman. ISBN: 9781580052597
- "The Principles of Successful Freelancing" by Miles Burke. ISBN: 9780980455243
- "Start and Run a Creative Services Business" by Susan Kirkland. ISBN: 9781551806075
- "Start Your Own Graphic Design Business" by Entrepreneur Press and George Sheldon. ISBN: 9781599181639
- "The Wealthy Freelancer" by Steve Slaunwhite, Pete Savage, and Ed Gandia. ISBN: 9781592579679
- "The Well-Fed Writer" by Peter Bowerman. ISBN: 9780967059877

Audio and Video Casts
- Escape from Cubical Nation Podcast: escapefromcubicalnation.libsyn.com
- Freelance Jam—Video Cast Show: freelancejam.com
- SmallBizPod Podcast: smallbizpod.co.uk

Learning New Skills
- A List Apart: alistapart.com
- CSS-Tricks: css-tricks.com
- Design Shack: designshack.net
- Smashing Magazine—Coding, Design, WordPress, etc: smashingmagazine.com
- Treehouse—Learn Design and Development for the Web: teamtreehouse.com
- Tuts+ Premium—Creative and Technical Skills: tutsplus.com

Free Portfolio Websites
- Behance: behance.net
- Big Black Bag: bigblackbag.com
- Bleidu: bleidu.com
- deviantArt: deviantart.com
- Carbonmade: carbonmade.com
- Coroflot: coroflot.com
- Krop: krop.com/creativedatabase
- Portfolio Box: portfoliobox.net
- Shown'd: shownd.com
- WordPress: wordpress.com
- Writer's Residence: writersresidence.com

Paid Portfolio Websites

- 4ormat: 4ormat.com
- Other Peoples Pixels: otherpeoplespixels.com
- Pixpa: pixpa.com
- Portfolio Box: portfoliobox.net
- ViewBook: viewbook.com

Communities and Professional Organizations

- AIGA: American Institute of Graphic Artists: aiga.com
- DevaintArt: devantart.com
- Forrst: forrst.com

Design Galleries

- Creattica: creattica.com
- Web Creme: webcreme.com

Acknowledgements

So many people helped me put together this book and who have been with me through my freelancing journey as a student, all of which deserve special thanks!

First and foremost, I must thank my amazing boyfriend, Steven Lassan. Thank you for being there every step of the way, not only through writing this book but also through everything in my freelancing career and most importantly, through everything during the past eight-plus years. Thank you for looking over my book several times and for taking the time out of your busy work schedule to thoroughly read and edit over 200 pages worth of content. I am so lucky and blessed to be with someone who is 1000% supportive of me no matter what (crazy) things I choose to do in life.

To my parents, thank you for not telling me to go get a "real" job. I hope I made you proud when I walk across that stage this past August.

To my professors at the Department of Art at Austin Peay State University, and most importantly to Barry Jones and Mark DeYoung for not thinking I was crazy (or thought I was crazy but didn't want to tell me). Between the two of you, I have grown so much as a graphic designer in my six years as an art student at APSU and find you both not only as amazing professors, but great mentors as well.

Big thank you to Joe Casabona and Daniel Francavilla for taking time to look over the earlier version of my book and giving me feedback as I started to finalizing the content to ready to publish. Also, a huge thank you to Laci Morgan and Daniel Francavilla (again) for helping me edit this book to make it final! Your input was invaluable during the publishing process and I greatly appreciate you all for taking time out of your busy schedules to look over what was the result of a school project!

Finally, none of my freelancing success and knowledge would have been developed if it wasn't for my wonderful clients I have had the absolute pleasure working with over the past five years of my freelancing career. Thank you for taking a chance on me and I hope I did not disappoint!

About the Author Amber Leigh Turner

Owner of January Creative, Amber has been a self-employed graphic and web designer for over five years, starting early in her collegiate career. Highly involved in all facets of design and marketing, Amber is passionate about design, marketing, freelancing (particularly as a student), and entrepreneurship.

Amber graduated from Austin Peay State University in Clarksville, Tennessee in August 2012 with two degrees: a Bachelor in Fine Arts in Visual Communications with a focus in Graphic Design, and a Bachelor of Business Administration in Marketing with a minor in Management.

Actively involved in the freelance community, Amber can be found in books and websites about freelancing, including the largest freelancing website *FreelanceSwitch* (freelanceswitch.com) and online tech and news site *The Next Web* (thenextweb.com). Freelancing as a student has given Amber the opportunity to start a student freelancing blog, appropriately named *Students That Freelance* (studentsthatfreelance.com) to help other students start freelancing during their collegiate years.

After graduation she continues to remain self-employed as the owner of January Creative to allow for the creative freedom enjoyed by the unique mixture of design, marketing, and solopreneurship. She also enjoys her solopreneurship by starting and managing new businesses soon to be launched.

You can learn more about Amber by visiting her personal website (amberturner.com) and her professional website of January Creative (januarycreative.com). She can also be found all over the Web on sites like Twitter (@amberlturner and @januarycreative) and Facebook (facebook.com/januarycreative).

Personal Notes

Have notes to add? You can add notes, thoughts, ideas, or anything else to these pages to help you stay organized. Use this section however you want!

30956716R00119

Made in the USA
Middletown, DE
12 April 2016